LADY BEA MORGAN!

The Extension to the "Pastor's Wife Does Cry!"

A Memoir by Lady Bea Morgan

All scriptures are taken from the King James Version of the Holy Bible.

The events in the book are actual and factual. The names have been changed to protect the innocent and the guilty.

Edited by: Lynel Johnson & Kendra Koger

Cover Designed by Sheldon Mitchell of Majaluk & LaRahn Michael

Manufactured in the United States of America

Library of Congress Control Number: 2011941139

ISBN: 9780983486053

For information regarding discounts for bulk purchases, please contact Prioritybooks Publications at 1-314-306-2972 or rosbeav03@yahoo.com. You can contact the author at: ladybmorgan@yahoo.com

Table of Contents

Dedication

I dedicate this book to Pastor's wives who are suffering with foolishness in their homes and within their churches and are not in the position to share.

I dedicate this book to pastors with characteristics of Pastor Claxton William Morgan.

I decree and declare that this book will strengthen marriages and ministries. My marriage failed because I couldn't hold it together alone and I did seek help from spiritual counselors and the Lord. The ministry failed because Claxton couldn't hold it together alone. He needed help, but didn't seek it diligently. Therefore, if two really become one, allowing Jesus to be the head, anything is possible.

Whatever state your ministry is in; my prayer is that your members become more like the church Jesus is coming back for upon reading my book.

Whatever state your marriage is in; my prayer is that your relationship exemplifies the marriage God designed Adam and Eve's to be upon reading my book.

Introduction

Lady Bea Morgan, The Extension

My memoir covers many components of ministry. I share personal encounters of the emotional, mental and verbal abuse I endured from my husband and the church members. It is filled with laughter and teaching material for pastors, their wives, ministers, their wives and lay members.

My book was not written to lift me up or to magnify me, neither was it written to pull down pastors or my husband. It was written to remind readers that in this life, we shall have tribulation, but we are to be of good cheer and he who lives Godly in Christ Jesus shall suffer persecution. Regardless to what we are faced with, we must trust in Jesus, stand on His Word and always remember His promises.

Blessed be God, even the Father of our Lord Jesus Christ, the Father of mercies, and the God of all comfort, *II Corinthians 1:3.*

Who comforteth us in all our tribulation, that we may be able to comfort them which are in any trouble, by the comfort wherewith we ourselves are comforted of God, *II Corinthians 1:4.*

 do refer to my memoir entitled The "Pastor's Wife Does Cry!" When you see TPWDC, I am referring to the book.

She is more precious than rubies: and all the things thou canst desire are not to be compared unto her, *Proverbs 3:15.*

Pastor's wives who have been a tremendous blessing to me in the last few years by precious deeds, counseling, listening, kind words, sweet smiles, friendship, praying and just laughing, I thank you so much!

"Women of Wisdom"

Lady Tanika Baylor, St. Louis, MO

Lady Ida Baylor, St. Louis, MO

Lady Sharon Pierson, New Rochelle, NY

Lady JoAnn Nelson, St. Louis, MO

Lady Cassandra McDonald, Zanesville, OH

Lady Tiara Payne, St. Louis, MO

Lady Denise Battle, St. Louis, MO

Lady Mona Bryant, St. Louis, MO

Lady Ruby Harvey, St. Louis, MO

Lady Freddie Pettiford, Washington Park, IL

Lady Marie McDaniels, St. Louis, MO

Lady Angela Sanders, St. Louis, MO

Lady Audrey Grayson, St. Louis, MO

Lady Lisa Hayes, St. Louis, MO

Lady Fadrienne Green, Birmingham, AL

Lady Sherry Parker, Overland, MO

Lady Mary Julian Rice, St. Louis, MO

Lady Lynn Davis, St. Louis, MO

Lady Marilyn Coleman, St. Louis, MO

Lady Sheila Coleman, St. Louis, MO

Lady Deborah Allen, St. Louis, MO

Lady Doretta Stephens, St. Louis, MO

Lady Alice Williams, St. Louis, MO

Lady Bettie Coats, St. Louis, MO

Lady Tina Pettiford, Washington Park, IL

Lady Wanda Cummings, St. Louis, MO

Lady Linda Battle, St. Louis, MO

Lady Kristen Williams, St. Louis, MO

Lady Nina Jones, St. Louis, MO

Lady Candace Hurd, Mayfield, KY

Where no counsel is, the people fall: but in the multitude of counselors there is safety, *Proverbs 11:14*.

Many pastors have been a great blessing to me in the last few years. If you have counseled me, encouraged me, ministered to me, invited me to minister or allowed me to minister to your congregation, I thank you!

"MEN AND WOMEN OF DIRECTION"

Bishop Larry Baylor, St. Louis, MO

Bishop Terence Coleman, St. Louis, MO

Bishop Jesse Battle, St. Louis, MO

Bishop James A. Johnson, St. Louis, MO

Bishop Melvin Williams, St. Louis, MO

Bishop Ronald Payne, St. Louis, MO

Suff. Bishop Robert Buckner, St. Louis, MO

Suff. Bishop Derek Pierson, New Rochelle, NY

District Elder Robert Nelson, St. Louis, MO

District Elder Edward Payne, St. Louis, MO

District Elder L. J. Harvey, St. Louis, MO

District Elder Illona Dickson, St. Louis, MO

Pastor Marlon Baylor, St. Louis, MO

Pastor Ronald Bobo, St. Louis, MO

Pastor Victoria Brown, St. Louis, MO

Pastor James Coats, St. Louis, MO

Pastor Michael Fowler, St. Louis, MO

Pastor Lance Bryant, St. Louis, MO

Pastor Marvin Sanders, St. Louis, MO

Pastor Joyce King, St. Louis, MO

Pastor Bernard Brown, St. Louis, MO

Pastor DeVone Cruesoe, St. Louis, MO

Pastor Alonzo Green, Birmingham, AL

Pastor Ronald Stephens, St. Louis, MO

Pastor Randall Murphy, Houston, TX

Pastor Casey Hayes, St. Louis, MO

Pastor Lynn Mims, St. Louis, MO

Pastor Glenn Allen, St. Louis, MO

Pastor Jennie Pittman, Chicago, IL

Pastor Shaunton Williams, St. Louis, MO

Pastor George Hurd, Mayfield, KY

Co-Pastor Jeaneal Byrd, Kansas City, MO

Ointment and perfume rejoice the heart: so doth the sweetness of a man's friend by hearty counsel, *Proverbs 27:9.*

Thank you to all of my
personal friends and family

Josephine, Niecie, Regina, Joyce, Evangelist S. Mack, Jackie, Baby Girl, Corey Fuller, Rose, Cedric, David, Karen, Carletta, Mary, Pam, Pat, Mother Lovely, Mother Johnson, Mother Baylor, Mother Triplett, Mother Smith, Sister V. Baylor, Teah, Yoshica, Charlotte, Erica Ewing, E. Matthews, Deja, Emi, Minister J. Elliott, Judy Welch, Kuley, Sister Savage, Evangelist Donna Scott, Michael and Alice Hicks-Chikeleze, Rockin' Roger Mathews, Deacon and Sister L. Sams, Gerald Jones, Brandon, Dorothy, Tambra, Shyroun, Connie, Paula Bentley, Alma, Deacon and Sister P. Timmons, Saundra Jackson, Sam, Tyron, Joe, Brian, Djuan, Tracy, Pam, Sherree, Demetrius, Carol, D. Washington, Nina, Tewawn, Veronica, Shantell, Deacon and Sister R. Moore, Janice, Uri, Fred, Cassandra, Alvin, LaDonia, Ronald, Tiara, Darius, Faith, Tim, Jakia, Kim, Tonya, Calisia, Laticia, April, Precious, Joy, Ahnna, Rahn, Calvin, Ollie Milligan, Chahn, Pooh, Jada, Chardae, ShaRahn, Imani, Tony, John, Jonae, Ryan, Shaelynn, Haleigh, Autumn, Alisia, McKenzie, Lil Cal, Romeo, Freddie, Fredrick, Dominique, Songnai, Ion, Judah, Jotham, Halley, Dee-Diane, The Cooley, Shannon, Miller, Wallace, Franklin, Garrett, Davis and Pullen families, Reggie & Olwen, Aunt Edna, Uncle Jerry, Bonnie, Sharon, Christy, Jeanelle, Corey and Shanna!

Prelude

I am Lady Bea Morgan, the wife of Pastor Claxton William Morgan, former First Lady of Greater Power Pentecostal Church of ten long years. Claxton and I have been married for 15 years. We have separated, reunited and separated again. Pride can destroy ministries and marriages if it is not dealt with. In our case, it wasn't. I have suffered and made it through verbal, mental and emotional abuse with the help of the Lord. With much fasting, praying and meditation, I am still standing and I am still serving the Lord Jesus Christ.

I am grateful for my trials; without them, my relationship with Jesus would not be as it is. I carried my cross; therefore, according to the Bible, I am worthy of Jesus. And he that taketh not his cross, and followeth after me, is not worthy of me, Matthew 10:38.

I have fasted consistently since 1997 and learned that fasting attracts demons. The devil knows that through fasting, his tactics will be revealed. Therefore, he tries to distract us while we're fasting so that we are discouraged, which will cause us to give up our fast.

If you are fasting, I encourage you to complete it. I know you may be hurting, I know you may be crying, but it's going to hurt worse and you're going to cry longer if you stop fasting. You may be in a furnace and surely do I know how hot it is; know that Jesus is with you. When you come out of that heat, you're going to be a blessing to many.

When my husband stopped pastoring, that was the cool down of the furnace for me; that was my healing. Because I was not into titles and other Pastor's wives didn't know that, they thought that the beginning of my suffering was when I no longer held the title "First Lady." Of course they didn't know me personally.

My encounters as a pastor's wife that were made known unto the saints were trials, but they were not my first trials; they were my first "public" trials. You'll see as you continue reading.

When my tenure ended as a pastor's wife, instead of the Pastor's wives in the organization calling me for prayer or to check on me, they were trying to figure out whether or not I had a nervous breakdown but pretending that all was well or if my joy was genuine. My tears of hurt were shed during my tenure as a pastor's wife, not afterward; I was set free! God did it!

But the God of all grace, who hath called us unto his eternal glory by Christ Jesus, after that ye have suffered a while, make you perfect, stablish, strengthen, settle you, *I Peter 5:10*.

No one enjoys suffering, but if there is good in suffering, we ought to look forward to our next trial.

Pastor's wives need a meeting place where they can go to ventilate, cry, share, and to bring their troubles; not to focus on the problems, but to focus on the healing, deliverance, restoration, comfort and peace of mind.

The tears of the pastor's wife aren't always of hurt and pain. She sheds tears of joy, tears of praise, tears of thanksgiving, tears of worship and tears of complexity. Nevertheless, the "Pastor's Wife Does Cry!"

Not only does the pastor's wife need a ventilation system, so do pastors. Claxton did not have a mentor. I believe that if the pastors who were supposedly overseeing the church, had taken time to oversee it, communicated with me, and counseled us, our ministry and marriage would have been different.

Claxton sold some of the church's property to offset church bills and he was accused of stealing money. The founder's children of Greater Power Pentecostal church took Claxton to court. The judge threw the case out. Then another attorney was hired because they were so sure that Claxton was in error. This angered the judge even the more and he threw the case out again. The bi-laws of the organization that we were in clearly stated that pastors have full control of the ministry's finances. I must say that Claxton loved the church he pastored and the members. What he did steal was time and money from his family to give to the church and the members. Rumors spread throughout the organization that Claxton stole money; how embarrassing.

Of course people thought that since we were married, I had to be a part of this scandal. In actuality, I had no knowledge of church business. Since Claxton was not able to be sued nor proven to be a thief, the District had no grounds to remove him from the pastoral position. When the church was financially struggling, Claxton should have asked for help from the entire staff and church instead of trying to handle it with just two of his deacons, but it didn't happen that way. Anyway, I received a telephone call from one of the higher echelon pastors stating that he needed to see me immediately; this was an emergency meeting. When I arrived, another pastor and one of the founder's children were also in attendance. All I thought was, "Three against one." I knew that Jesus was with me; therefore, I knew that if Jesus was for me, He was more than the world against me. The founder's child said that their car was parked in another area hidden from me to trick me so that I wouldn't have been deterred from attending. Was that deception? Prior to the meeting, I had a meeting with the Bishop concerning my marriage; counseling. He told me that this was a matter that he wanted to personally handle and instructed me not to tell anyone else about it. This meeting was only between the two of us. Then he told me to expect a call from him. Lo' and behold, this is when I received the call about the emergency meeting. Let me finish the story. So, the pastor in the meeting asked me to tell him what was going on with my husband. First of all, I am private, let's get that understanding. Secondly, the founder's child was hollering saying, "Tell them, tell them, tell them how your husband is!" During that quiet moment, when everyone was looking at me, waiting on my response, the Lord spoke to me and told me what to say. Somebody say, "The Lord spoke." I said, "My husband suffers with depression." The pastors looked at each other, frowned up, looked at each other again and said, "We can't ask Pastor Morgan to step down from pastoring due to depression. We can't do that." I was set up. The devil thought that I was going to share my marital troubles with them. This way, it would have been documented that Lady Bea was responsible for her husband being asked to step down as pastor. The plan didn't work. Then I asked if the two pastors in attendance would meet with Claxton and me without the founder's child. A meeting occurred later the same evening. We met and had prayer. Claxton had already moved out of our home. It's not a sin to separate from your spouse. There was really nothing that could have been done, but what was done; prayer. I did not call Claxton into the pastoral arena and certainly, I was not going to be the one to have him called out of it. It was a trick; it was deception in the morning and deception in the evening. Claxton resigned; it was a forced resignation. His name was torn up; his integrity was shot. This was the time when the pastors should have come together in prayer and fasting. Depression is a serious matter. When something like this happens to a leader and no counseling is offered and no apology or encouragement is given, he could stroke out. The carnal-minded are probably saying that Claxton got what he deserved. The spiritual-minded are probably saying, "Vengeance is Mine saith the Lord, I will repay." Meaning, whatever Claxton did or whatever people said

XIII

that he did, the spiritual-minded will pray. The spiritual-minded speaks life and peace and they know the Lord knows how to raise up a king and how to pull one down without assistance.

By the way, the Bishop never did call me. I called him and told him that deception was on every hand within the District. When we read in the Bibl "the Lord said," it came to past, regardless to whom He was talking to. This is how we are to be. We ought to be known as men and women of our word. A "kept" promise is greater than "a" promise. A "kept" word holds greater power than "a" word. The Bishop didn't keep his word, which disappointed me. We must keep our promises and our word, especially with sheep. Then I thought, maybe he forgot that the meeting we had together was private and maybe he forgot to call me, too.

Pastor's wives, whatever you're faced with in your marriage, the Lord sees it. He is our all-seeing eye God. However your husband is behaving, the Lord knows about it. He is all-knowing. Let the Lord fix it. I know that you can't speak about it, especially if your husband pastors a mega church and he is on television, Internet, radio, and travelling the world. Know that Lady Bea was where you are. Know that peace is coming. Know that you are not alone. Know that there are so many hurting Pastor's wives who are suffering inside. Know that I understand how it is to be obligated to do when you don't feel like doing. Know that the Lord is on your side! I am working on something

special for hurting women, especially the pastor's wives so
hold on!

LADY BEA MORGAN

The Extension to the ""Pastor's Wife Does Cry!""
A Memoir by Lady Bea Morgan

Chapter 1

My Most Memorable Christmas Present!

Christmas is my favorite holiday. I get excited about preparing for it. I usually take sweet potato pie orders from my siblings, cousins, friends and friends of friends. I bake no less than 50 pies; maxing out at about 150 pies. This doesn't include pecan pies and cakes, all from scratch. I love it! Some I'd sell, but most of the pies I'd give away. For some reason, as my family members were leaving the designated dinner location, Mama's, my sister's or my home, they took pies with them as if we had discussed it; I got used to it. I love Christmas decorating and picking out live trees the day after Thanksgiving. I place fruit, nuts and candy all over the house. I cook big dinners, everything from scratch; nothing instant. I love shopping for Christmas gifts and wrapping them, then hiding them. I'm getting excited thinking and writing about it all. Well, let me share my most memorable gift ever and if I was a betting woman, I'd bet that you can't top this gift, being the giver of the gift or being the recipient of the gift; you cannot beat it.

After my children opened all of their Christmas gifts in 2006, threw away the wrapping paper and cleaned the living room back up, it was time for my gift. My husband called me downstairs to his office. Stop hating, I'm feeling you! So when I entered his office, guess what he said?

He said, "You need a plan. You need a job or something. Your husband is leaving you." He then extended his arms, making outward circular motions with his hands while looking up at the ceiling and said, "All this, everything in my name is going to be cut off, disconnected lights, gas, phone, cable, all this is gon' be cut off. Merry Christmas, Merry Christmas from your husband. Your husband is leaving you. Merry Christmas, from your husband." He said this through his teeth. You know how you hold your teeth together and speak? I was so hurt. Not because he merely said that he was leaving me. Not even because of the fact that his plan was to leave me. I was hurt because he desired to steal my joy. He desired to destroy my happiness. He thought that since Christmas was my favorite holiday, he'd wait until that day to be sure that it was ruined. And guess what? It worked, he won and he destroyed my happiness. I have not celebrated Christmas since. Claxton William Morgan had forgotten that I was a praying and fasting woman and that my strength comes from the Lord. He had forgotten that my happiness could be tampered with, but not my joy. He desired to steal my joy, but couldn't. Happiness is based upon good things that happen. As long as life is great, happiness is at hand, but when trouble is present, happiness dissipates. The spirit of happiness controls your emotions because you are consistently up and down as situations present themselves. Joy is based upon what's within. With joy, regardless to the speed, dips, turns, or hills of the roller coaster of life, you continue to trust and depend on the Lord. When Jesus lives inside of us and we are in constant commune with Him,

He'll speak peace; comforting and guiding us regardless to the detriment of our trouble. With joy, you won't lose your hair, your mind, your energy, your money, your appetite, or your sleep. You can still laugh, crack jokes, counsel others, praise, worship, focus, and celebrate without planning revenge. My joy comes from the Lord; therefore, man can't take it away because man didn't provide me with it. The joy of the Lord is my strength.

I went upstairs, got on the phone and began calling the church members, wishing them a Merry Christmas as I always did. When they asked me about the gifts I received from the pastor for Christmas, I told them everything he gave me; just as he presented it. It was my present, he gave it to me, I shared it with his members and he heard me. He was just looking at me. I told you if I was a betting woman, I would have won this bet; you didn't believe me. Some of the members were in tears, some were angry, some were speechless. Though I stopped celebrating the Christmas holidays, I have learned that I can do without a tree of lights, but I cannot do without the tree of life, Jesus Christ. For years, I thought that I had to spend countless hours shopping, wrapping gifts, and decorating for Christmas. I have learned that the holidays are no longer first priority. Some years, I will celebrate, some years I won't. It will be my decision. Please don't think that I think I'm so hard whereas nothing affects me. Remember, The "Pastor's Wife Does Cry!" I am she! Lady Bea Morgan!

Claxton didn't move out right away. He moved out

the following April. The week before he left, he began
cleaning out his closet in the bedroom as I was lying on
the bed. Instead of him saying, "I'm moving this weekend"
or "I found an apartment," he said, "You ain't got to be no
rocket scientist to see that I'm getting out of here." Two
of my kids and I returned from church service one night
and witnessed a moving truck in the driveway. He was
scuffling, trying to carry his furniture. When one of my
sons saw the truck as he was walking home, that affected
him; he kept walking. My youngest son helped him. As
Claxton was moving, I was in peace. Had I not been with
Jesus; not just that evening, but, had I not been in His
Word and in His presence on a regular basis, I probably
would have caused a scene. I was on the phone while
he was moving, talking to one of my friends. As he was
disconnecting the cable box, I asked him, "Did the Lord
tell you to move?" He stopped unscrewing the screw,
looked up at me and said, "I don't know, but I am leaving."
I said, "As long as the Lord told you, you ain't got nothing
to worry about." He was so mad at me. I guess I acted or
reacted incorrectly. It wasn't he who was mad, it was the
devil. He told me that if I followed him to his new home,
he'd call the police on me for harassment. Can you believe
that? I have never followed him anywhere. Here he was,
leaving his family and his concern was me following
him. I learned later that his concern was not me knowing
where he was moving to; he didn't want me to see who
was helping him on the other end. It was Airika! Y'all
remember Airika? She was the lady who Claxton picked
up every morning before work so that she could use our

car all day.

I am trying to wrap up my most memorable Christmas present so that I can move on. Remember this is a memoir, not a novel. With a memoir, I can move around and not necessarily write in chronological order. So when you see a dash at the beginning of a paragraph, it indicates a new thought or memory.

Anyway, I started my plan as Claxton suggested. I got a part-time job, working for my book publisher and I wrote The "Pastor's Wife Does Cry!" in seven days. As my precious husband promised, as we know, he is a man of his word, he disconnected my cell phone. Because I was a step ahead of him, I had already ordered cell phone service and filed the order number. My service was restored within 30 minutes. Then I was led to change all of the other services to my name. Lo' and behold, my precious husband had planned to have all services disconnected on Friday evening, the Memorial Day weekend. I was supposed to be in the dark and heat, with spoiled food, no stove, no barbeque, no holiday. He knew that I wouldn't get services on until Tuesday. Somebody say, "Listen to the voice of the Lord." Every utility customer service agent I spoke with was so mad at Claxton. Nothing was interrupted nor disconnected. My sister-in-law was overheard saying with excitement that my utilities were scheduled to be disconnected on Friday at 4:00 p.m. On the holiday, somebody say, "On Monday." Me and Jesus clowned on that grill. Somebody say, "Claxton drove by." I wasn't barbequing, I was smok'n! He saw the smoke in the backyard from the front of the house, rising up like a glory cloud or like burnt offerings in the Bible and was furious.

Claxton's first wife left him and he was devastated. He brought that bitterness to our marriage, though it was hidden. In heated discussions, he'd threaten to leave me because he knew the detriment of the act. He thought that I was going to be affected by his departure like he was by hers. Come on, y'all, I'm Lady Bea! With God on my side, I stand in adversity, I stand in fire, I stand in the midst of storms and I take no credit! I used to tell Claxton that my first husband left me and I made it and I didn't have the Holy Ghost then.

What a Christmas present! Stay with me; I have so much to tell you.

Chapter 2

Preparation for Ministry

As a little girl, I was quiet. I always heard this voice instructing me to do things and how to do things better. I couldn't tell anyone because I was shy; I kept it to myself. My parents were entrepreneurs; they owned and operated many types of businesses. The main business was a nursing home. When my mom interviewed potential employees, she'd call me into her office, introduce me to the prospect, and then tell me to go into the waiting room. I never understood why she wanted me to meet these people until I got older. She'd call me back into the room and question me about the person. I'd run it down to her; how that person behaved at home; if the person was nice or just pretending; and some things I was afraid to share because they were so bad and I was scared that I would get a whipping for saying. You know, we got the beat down with the extension cord had we said the wrong thing. Some stuff I didn't tell Mama. My mother used my gifts to help with her business. I knew stuff, I felt stuff, I had dreams, and I heard this voice. When I looked at the senior citizens, I would hear a voice telling me their background, their likes and dislikes. Then I'd overhear them talking and would hear them confirm what was told to me by "that voice." I remember my dad telling me to spoon-feed one of the clients and I had an attitude about it; of course he didn't know how I felt. "That voice" said to me, "You don't know who's going to have to feed you one day." That made me think twice and I found joy in feeding her. I was told by my dad that the senior citizens were in their second state of childhood. He said that we were considered the same age. By him telling me this, I was more comfortable with them. We argued like siblings, especially over the television. Mary liked Lawrence Welk and I didn't. We kept changing the station back and forth until I heard "that voice" saying, "You have more time than her to watch television." I never changed the channel again and I began to enjoy the show.

- As a teenager, my cousin shared a story with me about a guy who had an artificial leg and girls were not interested in him because of it. I told her that I would be his friend. He started visiting me and it was a task getting adjusted to his one leg. I prayed and asked the Lord to help me with this adjustment. I asked the Lord to make me comfortable around him so that his disability was meaningless to me. I asked the Lord to fix it so that his wooden leg would not come between us. I asked the Lord to make our friendship special and to make us the best of friends. The Lord heard me and He honored my prayer. He was so nice and so comical. We began dating and we were so close just like I asked. I was crazy about him. This guy broke up with me and I almost lost my mind; literally. I cried and cried and cried for three days, all day and all night. He didn't have a good reason to break up with me. I didn't know what to do. That powerful voice said, "Reverse the prayer." It was so clear. I had to think about it.

Reverse the prayer. When I got that revelation, it was all over. I thought about every prayer I prayed for him or for us and reversed it. I remember saying, "Lord, remove him from my mind; from my system. Take the love that I have for him away from me. Remove every memory of him from my mind." When I got through with that prayer, I was free, free from him. The voice told me that he'd be back to apologize to me. When he came to my house, I opened the door and I was surprised to see him. Every feeling that I had for him was gone. He did apologize as the voice said. He was married. I was free from him. The Lord showed me the power in prayer as a teenager. When I see his sister at our class reunions, I tell her to be sure to thank her brother because it was him who started my prayer ministry. I had no pastor, no church and no spiritual director. God did it! If you're in a difficult situation, I encourage you to put the book down right now and reverse the prayer!

- Later on, I was introduced to alcoholic beverages; mixed drinks. I kept bottles in my purse and in my bedroom closet and nobody knew. The devil made me think that there was power in alcohol. The more he told me that, the more I bought, the more I drank and the more I thought I needed it. It gave me freedom to speak that which was on my mind regardless of the consequences. Remember, I was quiet. I kept my drinks in McDonald's cups while attending Business School. I had a dream that the dean found out about my gin and vodka and I was put out of school. Of course I stopped drinking at the school, but I didn't quit. What did happen was I was in typing class and could not type; I drank as the students typed. When I stopped drinking at school, a miracle happened. During the typing drills, the Lord made my typewriter keys sound like music to my ears. No one else could hear it but me. Within a few weeks I was typing 70 to 80 words per minute with three or less errors. The instructor said I cheated so she had me retake the drill as she stood over me. She couldn't believe it; neither could I. The Lord blessed me with a job as a secretary for the United States Department of Defense. Of course I didn't realize that it was the Lord's doing. I had taken the Civil Service test while I was pregnant with my first son. The application asked my availability for employment. My baby was due in May, so I wrote July. I had forgotten all about the test and the job. In July, the government called me for three interviews with three different departments in the same day. On my way home, I spoke with authority which position I wanted and sure enough, that was the department that offered me the job; learning about helicopters, how exciting! I never thanked the Lord. Isn't that how we do? I was now typing over 100 words per minute and never thought to thank the Lord.

- I used to go to the clubs every weekend. Before going, I made sure that I had plenty of gin or vodka inside of me. I wasn't a dancer; I listened to the music and watched the table, purses and drinks. While I was there, that powerful voice used to speak to me. "You could have been cleaning out your closet." In the midst of the smoke, loud music, a lot of people, and the alcohol in me, the Lord spoke to me. He'd say things like, "This is fun?" The words really made me think. Every time I went out, the more I heard from the Lord. I decreased my partying by eliminating one weekend for a month or two, then two weekends for a month or two. Eventually, I stopped going. I can't sleep during the daytime, so when I'd get home from the club, I'd stay up until the next night. That was killing me. I had a baby and I had to be at work on Monday. I was taking medicine to stay awake at work. I was dealing with spiritual warfare and didn't know it. The devil was pulling me to the alcohol and to the club and the Lord was speaking to me at the club. When I couldn't sleep after returning home from the club, I read Proverbs and I was too ashamed to tell my best friend about it. In fact, in route home from the club, there was nothing on the radio but Gospel music at that hour on Sunday morning. I needed to hear some R&B. There I was riding home, full of alcohol and listening to real Gospel music that convicted me. You know the Gospel music that you hear that you don't have to wonder if it's Gospel or not? You know that kind of music where the anointing makes you repent? That was the music I rode home to. I thought it was awful then, but I was spiritually blind. That was good Gospel music!

- I started having dreams that were spiritually affecting me. I was always a dreamer and my dreams always came to pass like my grandma being killed by "the" people and years later, in actuality, her doctor prescribed penicillin to her while she was in the hospital. She was allergic to penicillin and it was documented in her records. Her body burned up from the inside out and she died. The people were the nurses. These dreams were scary to me. I had a dream that I needed to pay tithes to my church because the church was experiencing electrical problems and needed my money. The dream directed me to write a check to them as soon as I got paid. When I woke up, I meditated on the dream because it was so clear and strong. It was also payday, I didn't have a church home and I didn't know what tithes were. The voice told me how much to write the check for and to write it to the church I grew up in. I did just that. A couple of months later I shared it with my parents and my Mom called the pastor. As soon as he heard my mom's voice, he told her about the electrical problems and how my check helped with the repairs; he was so grateful. I had a dream that my mom passed away after my son graduated from high school. When I had the dream, my son was a baby. I was so excited about my son graduating; I didn't focus on her death because that was so many years ahead. You know how young people live? They live for right now or for today. Then I had another dream that my grandma told me that she was taking her sister and my dad with her; remember, my grandma had passed away. I asked her to leave my Dad, but she could take her sister. She said that she was taking them both. In actuality, I was sharing that with my parents, but not the whole dream; just the part about my mom's aunt passing. My mom called her aunt and told her that I had something to tell her. I stood in her bedroom, waved my hand and said in a whisper, "Nah, Mama, I ain't telling her that." Mama said, "Come on, get the phone, gal." I said, in rhythm with my hands, in a whisper, "I am not telling her that, Mama." My aunt said, "I already know." Mama said, "You already know what?" She said, "Bea came into my room and told me in a vision that she was coming for me." Bea was my grandma's name, too. So my Dad asked me, "Did she say anything about me?" I lied and said no because I was afraid to tell him the truth. Surely, they died. My dad died first in April, which was a few weeks after the dream, and my aunt died the following month. My mom passed away, too, 17 years after my dream I had about her. My son graduated high school the first week of June and she died June 29 just like my dream prophesied. The Lord was speaking to me more and more through dreams. I didn't understand what was going on.

- I moved into my apartment and was determined to dig more into the Bible. The Lord instructed me to buy a Bible on payday with a leather cover and to have my name engraved on it. I did just that. At night, I attempted to read it, but couldn't because I couldn't stay focused. When I read four or five words, my electric bill would flash before me. I'd read a little more, then something that happened at work flashed before me. Then the gas bill would come before me; the due date. If I remembered a past due bill, I'd get nervous, get my checkbook and as I'd pass by the bathroom, I'd say, "Let me clean the bathroom up right quick." When I'd finally make it back to the dining room table I'd say, "I'll read some more tomorrow, I'm going to sleep." This went on everyday and it started getting tiresome. Here's what I did. I'm trying to live holy, right? So I had already stopped drinking the hard drinks. Thanks be unto God, I was not an alcoholic; I just loved my drinks and could tolerate a lot of it. It was easy for me to put it down. However, I bought beer and wine coolers to drink while I read my Bible. I could concentrate on what I was reading and understood what I was reading. My mind was off of my troubles. I went to the liquor store daily, right after work. After weeks of this technique, drinking and reading the Bible, the drinking decreased as my understanding of the Bible increased. Eventually, I no longer needed to drink because I was growing stronger and could focus. Years later, I found a scripture that gave me understanding of my drinking and reading the Bible. Give strong drink unto him that is ready to perish, and wine unto those that be of heavy hearts. Let him drink, and forget his poverty, and remember his misery no more, Proverbs 31:6-7. I had given up the strong drinks, but that which I did drink allowed me to forget my troubles temporarily. I am not advocating this formula as a means of you drawing closer to the Lord.

- I married a gentleman by the name of Ricky and we were equally yoked. At that time, I had no knowledge of what being equally or unequally yoked meant. We were both out of the will of the Lord. We were both still sinning with no spiritual guidance. I did have some advantages; I had spiritual gifts. I was a dreamer, I listened to Gospel music, radio preachers, and I read the Bible. I did not have a church home or pastor. God was calling me and I didn't realize it. Ricky accepted an over-the-road truck driving position which opened many satanic doors to our marriage. He would never call to tell me when he was in route home; he'd surprise me. The Lord would tell me though I didn't know that it was the Lord. I always told my friend when Rick was coming home. When he arrived, I would be awake and sitting up; I was expecting him. He was mad because I knew when he was coming home and he couldn't surprise me. He said that a voice couldn't have told me. He hated when I mentioned scriptures. One day he slammed my kitchen radio on the floor because he didn't want to hear my church music. He broke it and the Gospel station was the only channel it could get. That scared him and he promised never to throw my stuff again. He was an observant husband. If I left the house with lipstick on, I'd better have some on when I returned or he'd question it. He thought every man wanted me. Six feet tall, wearing size nine clothes, was not cute to me. I never thought that thin was in. I wanted to be heavy. He thought that men were double looking me. I had nothing to be looked at twice. I couldn't understand him. He called me Beatrice. Well, one Saturday night I bought a hot dress, not hot off the press and not hot as in fire as the kids say, but hot as in stolen. I got it for $20 and it was nice. I was determined to go to church in the morning. As I was getting dressed, I said, "I'm getting dressed for Jesus." I didn't even know what I was saying. Everything was perfect that day; my outfit, my stolen outfit at that, my hair, and my shoes. When I got to church, I got comfortable on my pew. It seemed as if the pastor gave altar call as soon as I got there. I wanted him to go on with the service; after all, I was dressed for Jesus in my hot outfit. I wanted Jesus to see me. The pastor kept going on and on, encouraging the lost to come to Jesus. The choir was singing "Come to Jesus While You Still Have Time." The pastor finally ended altar call and went back to his seat. I was glad he sat down because during that time of the service I always felt like crying and I felt as if I was sinning, which I was. I liked when all of that was over. I just wanted to go to church, hear the choir, put some money in the offering basket as if I was doing something great, stomach through the sermon, and then go home; nothing more. The pastor got right back up. I was thinking that I was safe, why did he get back up? I was tired of holding my cry; that hurts.

He came to the section where I was seated. I couldn't believe how this pastor was getting on my nerves; my face was in turmoil from straining, trying to keep my composure. I was thinking, "What is wrong with him?" He said, "The Holy Ghost said that there is one more to come to Jesus and the person is in this area. You may be scared to come, you may be shy. If you're shy, just raise your hand and the usher will come and get you." At that time, a hand went up in my row. I looked down the pew, being nosey because I wanted to see exactly who it was; not that I knew them, I was a visitor. I looked at everyone's face and hand in my row, one by one. It was my hand that went up in the air. I tried to pull it down and it wouldn't come down. I even used my other hand to pull it down and couldn't. By that time the usher was there to escort me. I had to walk in front of all those people and I don't even remember the walk; the Lord had me. In the natural, the usher had my hand, but in the spiritual, Jesus had it. I was baptized that day. I was afraid of water, but the Lord removed the fear of water from me. I vaguely remember being immersed. The pastor had no idea that he was calling to the altar the future pastor's wife of his best friend's church. Remember, I left home with my hair in curls. When I got baptized, my hair got wet so I had to go home with my hair slicked back. I said to myself, "I have to deal with this crazy man." I didn't know what I was going to say about my hair; how could I explain that? The Lord knew. My husband said nothing; he hadn't noticed. The Lord took care of it.

I was worried for nothing. I still didn't have a church home and don't know why I didn't join that church, which was Bethesda. I was trying to live right. I had no mentor and had no saved friends. My nieces and nephew were saved and attended their dad's church; he was the pastor. I didn't think that I was welcomed there because the pastor was my sister's former husband. Besides, my nieces and nephew couldn't teach me about the Lord, surely they knew not much in my eyes. I was the auntie. They were supposed to learn from me not me learn from them.

- One day I went to the store and as I was getting out of the car I saw on the floor a bag that belonged to Ricky. The Lord said, "Open it." I said, "Lord, You know I don't ramble." "Open it." "No, Lord." Once more, with great authority, He said, "Open it!" I opened it and there were telephone numbers of women from all over the United States and Canada written on torn-off brown paper bags, matchbook covers, newspaper, construction paper and every color paper in the Crayola box. I was flipping through the numbers and was amazed at the behavior of a married man. As I flipped through the numbers, the Lord said, "Stop, write this number down." I copied the name, number, address and work number. The Lord said, "Put it in your wallet." I did just that and never got upset. I never told him about it and actually, I forgot about it. It seemed as if everything went wrong once I got baptized and tried to live holy, though I was not delivered from my habits and ways yet. At that time, I did not know that the voice I heard and followed was that of the Lord's. I had been following "that" voice since childhood. It wasn't until I was older that I learned who had been speaking to me all those years.

- We had one car and I learned that it was used to transport drugs by my husband when he was in town. Ricky was using and selling crack cocaine, wasn't that beautiful? I couldn't believe it. When he got paid, he'd smoke the whole check up and then he'd cry about it. Between him and me, I don't know who cried the loudest. What I did know was that we had bills and kids. He didn't pay the bills or the sitter, I did. He did cook and clean when he was home. Instant replay in slow motion! He did cook and clean when he was home.

- My car stopped on me and the warranty was expired. What was I going to do? I had to go to work and I had the kids and we had no money. I had a mechanic come by to check it out and the quote almost killed me. I was sitting in my car thinking, not praying, when a man pulled up in a car beside me whom I did not know and said, "Leave your car where it is and I will pick it up, take it to my house, put it in my garage and fix it. I won't charge you a dime, I will protect it and you can pick it up on Sunday evening." I had nothing to lose, it didn't work anyway. I couldn't believe it. It happened just like he said. My car was like new. I learned later

that he was a known dealer, not a car dealer, in the
area. God wanted me to know that if I kept trying
to live holy that He'd bless me. Then I received an
eviction notice for not paying rent and I had 30 days
to vacate the premises. I had all of my receipts. It
was a lie; what an inconvenience. Somewhere in all
of the turmoil I had a dream that my best friend and I
had stopped talking without a cause and it happened.
Meanwhile, my son was asthmatic. Three to four
times per week, I rushed him to the emergency room
for breathing treatments. When I'd get to the hospital,
I'd leave my oldest son in the car while I charged into
the hospital with my baby, bypassing paperwork and
giving insurance info to save his life. When the people
saw me running in, they ran towards me to snatch my
child out of my hands. Then I rushed to get my oldest
son out of the car; he'd be asleep. He was five years
older and in school. In the midst of all this, somebody
say, "The Lord said." The Lord said, "Get the number
and call." Remember the woman's telephone number
that I had put in my wallet? I called, a lady answered
and said, "Ricky is not home, is there a message?" I
was so outdone I just told her there was no message.
I called again; she asked if there was a message.
Again, I told her there was none. I called again and
left a message for Rick to call his wife. The last time
I called another woman answered. I said, "May I
speak to Ricky, please?" She said, "Excuse me?" I
repeated myself, she repeated herself. I felt in the spirit
that her neck was rolling. I kindly repeated myself.

Then she asked, "Is something wrong with the kids?" Remember, all I did was get baptized. I didn't have the Holy Ghost yet. I had her address in Iowa. I was cool though. I didn't go North side on her. I may not have had the Holy Ghost, but the Holy Ghost was near. I said, "So if something is wrong with my kids, then I can speak to my husband?" She said, "Yeah." I was thinking that all I did was get baptized and everything crashed. She said, "I don't appreciate you calling my house, playing on my phone." I know what I wanted to say, but God gave me the words. I said, "If your husband was here with me and you called my house, I would let you speak to him. I'm not calling your husband or my boyfriend; I'm calling your house to speak with my husband." She was quiet for a while and began apologizing and told me everything from A to Z. She should have written a book. We talked a couple of hours. I learned something interesting. She paid her bills and gave Ricky, Slick Rick, the remainder of her check. I said, "Sweetie, that's why he's there with you and not here." One evening I received a call from a frantic woman; she was crying and needed help. This was the same lady, my husband's mistress, Kendra. I told her to get her Bible, which she didn't have. I ministered to her until she was under control. In fact, I ministered to her every time she called. When she bought a Bible, we had Bible class late at night while her man, my husband, was out. I didn't have a pastor and I didn't have a church home, but I had a friend in Jesus. I told her what He "that voice" told me to tell her. When Rick came home, I didn't have time to deal with all that lying, false promises and apologies. I had 30 days to move. One of those weekends, I had a visitation from the Lord. I was asleep and I felt a cool whistling wind in the bedroom. I was so scared. The voice said, "Don't be afraid, I'm just the Holy Spirit, I am going to take care of you." No one was there; I was shaking. I thought to myself that I was just dreaming and was so glad to be awake. There was an instant replay. The Lord was letting me know that I was not dreaming; this was real. During my sufferings, I comforted myself with those Words, "Don't be afraid I'm just the Holy Spirit, I'm going to take care of you." That same night I learned that Kendra was in town, staying the night at my mother-in-law's house with my husband. Neither of my in-laws, you know the ones who loved me so much, told me. Kendra told me herself once she returned home. I confronted my mother-in-law about the weekend visit and she told me that it was not her business who Rick was with; he was grown. I agreed with her one hundred percent that it wasn't her business about what he was engaged in. Then I told her that it was her business as to what transpires in her house. I told her that whatever she allowed to take place in her home, she was responsible for. I told her that if there was a drug bust in the home, the homeowner was going down, too. Everything that happens in our lives is a lesson. I learned how to handle my daughters-in-law when I get them. Should "any one" of my sons think that they are going to bring another woman to my house while married, they are in trouble. Prayerfully this does not happen. If my sons refuse to pay child support or keep their employment private, it wouldn't be a good idea for them to tell me because I'm telling! The following week, while I was packing, my belongings were coming up missing like my television, for instance. As I continued packing and moving things into my new home that was being repaired, a Greyhound bus ticket fell out of Rick's jacket pocket that he left in the car; he was leaving in a few days, going to Iowa. He was at his Mom's house when I decided to confront him about the ticket. My niece, Tiny decided to ride with me; she was 12 years old. When I arrived, my husband was walking with my son, Rich and they were holding hands. The devil told me to run my husband over with the car and if I hit him, my son would not be hurt. When that thought entered my mind, I moved on it. I put my foot to the floor and guess what happened? We were flying across the parking lot; pedal to the floor. Guess what happened, guess! Let me tell you. You know my niece, Tiny, the 12 year old? She started speaking in tongues in my backseat. Guess what happened? The Lord stopped the car. The devil in me was so mad. When I got home, I cussed Tiny out, good fashioned, as my grandma would say. Tiny didn't hear me cussing her out; she wasn't there. I couldn't believe she was speaking in tongues in my car. I couldn't understand why she jumped in my car in the first place. I was as hot as that stolen suit I had on when I got baptized. I was pacing the floor for hours, replaying the incident; me seeing Rick and Rich walking, me putting the pedal to the floor; Tiny saying, I'm riding with Bea; Tiny speaking in those tongues; why did she ride with me; why did she jump in my car? I kept repeating those lines for hours.

- When I went to the courthouse, I was sitting in the courtroom amongst a lot of people. As I looked across the room, I spotted an evil man. The Lord said, "That's the one who caused this." Our names were called and we stood before the judge and I proved that rent was paid. Though the landlord's son wanted me out of the apartment in 30 days, the judge gave me 60 days to move. I had already moved out and moved in with my brother until my home was available. Sure enough, the evil man that the Lord told me about while I was in the courtroom was my landlord's son.

- On page 8 of The "Pastor's Wife Does Cry!" (TPWDC), I mentioned that Satan only tests the strength of something and not the weakness. Let me explain what I meant by that. When the Lord chose me to live holy, I was tested greatly by Satan. My determination to serve the Lord was tested. I didn't turn back; I didn't give up on God. I realized that God moved me away from everyone who distracted me so that I could study His Word, grow stronger in Him and learn how to pray. The Lord was preparing me for ministry, though I didn't know it then.

I moved in with my brother and while living there I studied the Word of God every night after my kids were asleep. I had only taken two weeks of clothing with me because the house I was renting was being repaired and was going to be ready for occupancy in two weeks. When I stopped by the house to get more clothes for us, I learned then that the house was rat-infested. These were lowdown rats. We lost all our clothes, shoes, mattresses, sheets and everything chewable. I lost all my coats, including my furs; all of them. I stood in that house, shook my head and said, "Lord, this is probably how Job felt when he lost everything. You must have a blessing for me." He was preparing me for ministry. That lesson was two-fold. The first lesson was: Focus not on materials that can be replaced, broken, stolen, rotten, eaten or chewed on. *Lay not up for yourselves treasures upon earth, where moth and rust doth corrupt, and where thieves break through and steal: But lay up for yourselves treasures in heaven, where neither moth nor rust doth corrupt, and where thieves do not break through nor steal: For where your treasure is, there will your heart be also, Matthew 6:19-21.* The second lesson was: Before moving all my belongings into an empty house, give the house a "rat" test. Leave a mink coat in the house for two weeks. If it's shredded, don't move anything else in. Those two weeks of study time at my brother's house turned into months of study. I became stronger in the Lord. One Sunday I was listening to a church service on the radio and it blessed me. The following Sunday I called for directions to the church. I didn't visit the church until the first Sunday of the following year. That was the beginning stages of Greater Power Pentecostal Church where I met Elder Claxton William Morgan. I do detail the beginning stages of our relationship and engagement in TPWDC. Right before Claxton and I got married, Kendra called me. Remember her? She was Ricky's girlfriend. She said that she had been trying to contact me for such a long time and couldn't reach me. She said that there was one more number in the phone book with my first name initialed and my last name spelled out. She was so excited to hear my voice, but I had forgotten her name and who she was. My phone was scheduled to be disconnected the next day. She called to apologize to me for dating my husband. She said, "I knew it was wrong, but I really know how wrong it was now that I am saved, sanctified and Holy Ghost filled." She thanked me for the Bible classes we used to have on the phone. She thanked me for my Gospel music that ministered to her. Ricky would take my cassette tapes and record rap music over them. Well, some of those tapes didn't get recorded over. The Lord used Ricky to drive my tapes that he took from me, my favorite songs, to Kendra in Iowa. Then she thanked me for some prophesies that came to pass in a letter I wrote to her. One prophecy was that she'd gain full custody of her children once she lived for the Lord. With excitement she said, "I have full custody of my children just like you said! They are in church now and I sing in the choir!" Then she said, "I have that light! I have it now!" "Light?" I asked. "Yes," she responded. "You told me in a letter that I was blinded by Satan's 10,000-watt light, but as soon as I get Jesus' 75-watt light that I would see things clearer, I got that light! I got it! Thanks to you! Don't you remember?" I remembered once she mentioned it to me. Ricky told his Mom that he hated when I spoke to any of his girlfriends because they always broke off the relationship with him to either be saved or to come out of the backslidden state to be back with Jesus. Ricky and I never reunited, but he did write me a long letter of apology, expressing the errors he made as a husband and a father and how sorry he was for leaving a wife who loved him. He was angry at himself for the decisions he made and the years he wasted. He regretted missing out on raising his sons. To date, he has been given an opportunity to meet and develop a relationship with his children and they do communicate.

- In between the time the Lord called me to the ministry and accepting the call, I got extremely sick. I had a fever for weeks that over-the-counter medicine couldn't control. I lost so much weight because I wasn't eating. Did you ask me why? Well, I was too weak to cook. Did you ask me where Claxton was? Ah, he was gone doing ministry work. Who cooked for Claxton? He brought dinner home, wasn't that nice of him? He brought "din-ter" home for himself, smelling up the bedroom. I thought you asked me if he offered me some. Not a fork full, not a grain, not a morsel, and I was too weak to ask for some. Our soiled clothes were piled up as high as Mount Nebo and Claxton was still working the ministry. My doctor made arrangements for me to be admitted into the hospital. In route there, a Word dropped into my spirit that I was sick due to not preaching His Word as He asked. I promised the Lord that if He made me well that I'd preach in spite of what Claxton told me. Claxton said that I was not called and that I'd never preach in his pulpit. During my four-day stay in the hospital, I was diagnosed with liver trouble, dehydration, low potassium and spleen issues with no appetite. Well, who fed my kids while Claxton was doing ministry work? Let me answer that. Claxton's first wife went to my house and fed my children for me. Wasn't that nice? Ladies, get to be friends with your husband's former wife or your former husband's wife. You really could be a help one to another while connecting a blended family peacefully. Why can't the kids see the two of you getting along and on one accord? My stepchildren were not allowed to talk about me in a negative way when they returned home from the alternating weekend stays at my house. They didn't discuss their mom in a negative way with me either. She bought me gifts, gave me money, gave me recipes, she ate my food, we fasted together and helped each other; Claxton couldn't understand it. Anyway, the doctors said I had a virus that had to run its course.

The Lord healed me and I kept my promise which was to preach.

Chapter 3

The Origin of Ministry Destruction

In the Intro of TPWDC book, I mentioned how Claxton was introduced at church by the announcer. When he graced the podium, he'd say, "God bless you wonderful Saints, but now I want you to give the Lord praise." Let me interject right here for just a moment. I believe that it was during this time when the spirit of pride rested upon him. He started thinking that he was great. Pride was the origin of the destruction of the ministry. I am complimentary by nature; I encourage others without thought. When I see something I like, I compliment it. When someone does great deeds or acts, I express it in words. I utilize wisdom when doing so because compliments can be interpreted incorrectly. I don't want a woman to ever think I'm flirting with her husband or a man to ever think I'm flirting with him, especially while I'm married. I want to always be in the position of trustworthiness. If I don't like something, I won't tell you unless you ask or unless I'm led of the Lord. Please don't ask me, please don't make me answer. I kept Claxton uplifted and feeling good. He used to tell me that he didn't have to worry about other women boosting his ego because his wife did an excellent job in that area (he was tested). Always expect a test after you decree something. To him, that was a law; a fact; a decree ("my wife does"). Then he spoke it, he told me; he made it known unto me; he declared it. If I say, "I really love the Lord." That's a decree; that's a fact. Because I decreed it, I am going to be tested. Who will test me? Well, The LORD trieth the righteous, Psalm 11:5 and Satan tried Job, with the Lord's permission. Our problem was when Claxton asked me about certain people, places and things like issues of the church, for instance, he expected me to say that all was well all of the time. Constructive criticism? No, that wasn't Claxton's best suit to wear. He wouldn't allow me to exercise my spiritual gifts. I had dreams, I had visions and the Lord personally informed me. When I shared it with him, he became angry. I thought that my gifts, coupled with his knowledge, talents and gifts would make us an awesome package deal for Jesus. That's what happens when we "thought" too much. I should have spent more time "thinking" and not "thoughting." I had to utilize wisdom as to when to share with him what thus said the Lord. Everything that happened to him, he was warned about it by Jesus through me. Lest Satan should get an advantage of us: for we are not ignorant of his devices, II Corinthians 2:11. When we are warned, we must take heed.

In the midst of all that, Claxton's chest began swelling, not from lifting weights, but from the lifting up of pride. Pride will cause one to be a heavyweight chump, not a heavyweight champ. Because Satan is so smooth and sly, he will have us walking in the spirit of haughtiness without us knowing it. He'll make us think that we are moving forward in Jesus, but in actuality, we are moving backward in slow motion. Claxton thought that he was greater in Jesus than me because he had been in church since childhood. I always knew that he was sharp with the Word; I was not competing with him and neither did I combat his teachings. I looked forward to hearing him teach and preach. He's a teacher by trade and excellent at it.

Pride caused Claxton to belittle me so that he could uplift himself. The devil is something. This was not only pride, jealousy entered as well. He stopped accepting my compliments; they were minor; minute; mini. He closed his ears slowly to my words of encouragement, but opened his ears widely and rapidly to the multitude of words from the people. Woe to the multitude of many people, which make a noise like the noise of the seas; and to the rushing of nations, that make a rushing like the rushing of mighty waters, Proverbs 17:12. They magnified his name, his works and his preaching. This caused my encouragement to him to be worthless and theirs worthy. I didn't stand a chance; my measly words standing against a district of churches, a congregation, radio listeners and television viewers. I witnessed Claxton's head enlarge in various areas. He'd say, "These people love me." He was spiritually blind and spiritually deaf. I'd say, "Claxton, don't focus on what the people say, these people carry the same spirit as those in Matthew who said, "Hosanna in the highest." These are going to be the same people to crucify you later." And whatsoever ye do, do it heartily, as to the Lord, and not unto men, Colossians 3:23. He couldn't hear me. When people speak, I recognize the spirit that rests upon the words as they flow into the atmosphere; the same with singers. I knew what I was saying to him was from the Lord.

As years passed, pride heightened along with other unrighteousness. When we are in error, the Holy Ghost will speak to us, lead us, and guide us. When we ignore the Lord, He will turn wise men backward, and make their knowledge foolish, Isaiah 44:25.

Chapter 4

My Unusual Prayers and Results

A pastor's wife, especially an abused pastor's wife, must stay in constant prayer. It is prayer that changes situations. It is prayer that changes us. When we travel down Trouble Terrace, Persecution Plaza, Trial Trail, Suffering Street or Infirmity Interstate, we don't know how long the road will be, but we must believe that our prayers are being heard, felt, and answered by Jesus Christ Himself. When the three Hebrew boys were in the fiery furnace in the book of Daniel, e-mail me or text me the length of time they spent in their trouble. My Bible didn't tell me or maybe I missed it. One thing for sure, my Bible does say that they were delivered. They believed in their God and this is what we have to do.

Pastor's wives silently cry out often, but it seems as if no one knows their requests. They scream in first soprano, but it's silent to the ears of the Saints. Well, silent to the supposedly deep, in-depth prayer warriors of my church. Oh, that's right, that's because my screams were silent; they weren't supposed to hear them. Seriously, if they were heard in the spirit, they were not made known to me.

I am sharing some of my personal prayers and concerns that I wrote in a notebook to the Lord as a new pastor's wife. This is between me and you, okay?

a. Dear God, please heal any hurts in my life concerning the way I feel about having an unloving husband along with feeling unprotected by my husband. Jehovah Rapha, You are my Healer and knowing this and believing the same, I will be healed.

b. It is impossible for me to set aside time for us to be alone and that is because he is so busy and he does not have a schedule enabling me to do so.

c. Lord, I feel that we are losing touch with one another. We are growing spiritually, but we have no time to share it with one another. He knows not much about me now. He still knows the one he married four years ago.

d. I believe my husband knows that he is first, after God, on my list of priorities. I believe that he puts everyone else before his family because he is a pastor and he is trying to assure his members that they can count on him at anytime, no matter the hour or the cause. I feel that he believes that his family will understand and that the family can wait because they will always be there, but members come and go; so while they (the members) are present, he will be there.

e. Dear God, please help me to see that my husband's priorities are in line with Your Word. Help me to understand that my husband's priorities are supposed to differ from mine. Lord, please show my husband the order in which he should live by and after showing him Your vision, direct him to me. Lord, show him that his family is before the church. Show him that the needs of his family are to be fulfilled first before he can take care of the needs of Your people. Show him that he must live by example and not just by dictation. Lord, please let him realize that childhood is a one-time thing and that his example of great fatherhood is to be displayed so that his children can adopt his ways. Lord, let him see that he is to enjoy his wife of his youth.

f. Lord, Your Word tells us that a good tree cannot bear bad fruit and a bad tree cannot bear good fruit. A tree bearing bad fruit will be cut down and cast in the fire. Lord, I ask that my husband bear good fruit out of the goodness that is within him and that he will know of the goodness that he does. May the fruit of honesty, trustworthiness and humility sweeten all his dealings so that his reputation will never be spoiled. Lord, preserve his busy life from the enemy. Hide him from the secret counsel of the wicked. Pull him out of any net that has been laid before him. Keep him safe from the mouths of gossipers. All those who are involved in the gossip, with the intent to slander his name, my prayer Lord is for You to touch their lips with Your finger and cause confusion in their lives. Where there has been ill spoken upon him, reveal the responsible party.

g. Dear God, keep us from the lips of gossipers. Lord,

when we enter their minds and as their lips form to speak about us, cause them to forget what they were going to say and should they remember again, speak to them Lord informing them that what they are about to say is untrue and ungodly. Let them know that the energy used to gossip can be used to edify You. Let them know that instead of spreading bad news; spread the Good News of You.

h. When my husband watches not what he says to me, it does not matter to him because it's "me" and he takes me for granted. I mean nothing to him at all, only in the presence of the saints. I make a perfect-looking "pastor's wife," but not his wife. What I mean is, I look the part of the perfect "pastor's" wife. I have that behavior, I have that look, "plain," I have the conversation of that perfect pastor's wife which makes him look good which is all that's important; not me nor my feelings, nor my opinion, nor my thoughts, nor my interests. It is all about him. The spirit of haughtiness crept upon him. But there is a God and as long as I am His servant, this pride will be cast down and will continuously stay down.

Surely all these prayers and concerns were heard by the Lord, they were sincere as well. I believed that Jesus heard me.

My fasting life was ever increasing back then. The more I fasted, the more the Lord revealed Himself to me. The more the Lord revealed Himself to me, the more Satan attacked me. The more Satan attacked me, the more I prayed. The more I prayed, the stronger I got and the bolder I got in Jesus. I didn't know much about the terms demonic forces, Satan's hold, strongholds, spirit realm, wickedness in high places, principalities, soothsayers, satanic dominions or warlocks. The Lord revealed it to me. The Lord taught me how to pray the scriptures, too. I borrowed a book on praying the scriptures. When I opened it, the Lord spoke. He said, "Don't read it, I will teach you." I never read it. I was led to go to Colossians. Once there, the Lord had me to write the verses out and insert "my, I, or my name" wherever I could. For years I had trouble memorizing scriptures. I took my concern to the Lord. One thing I love about my Lord is His Word, His promise that reads The LORD will perfect that which concerneth me, Psalm 138:8. The Lord told me that memorizing scriptures is not as important as reading the scriptures, remembering the revelation of the scriptures and living that which was revealed; how profound!

My prayers eventually changed as I grew spiritually. I stopped praying for my marriage, my husband, my church, my troubles and my kids. I began praying prayers of thanksgiving. Thanking God for what my husband does do. The more I thanked the Lord for what my husband did versus what he wasn't doing, the more my husband was clowning. The more he clowned, the more I prayed. The more I prayed, the more trouble I had coming at me faster than the whirlwind of a tornado. Trouble was on every hand every day. I had no time to focus on last week's dilemmas because this week brought me a new display of trials. I couldn't focus on yesterday's issues because I was dealing with today's drama. By this time, I had forgotten about last week's dilemmas and while storing up prayers preparing for tomorrow's brand new mercies, I mean tomorrow's brand new messes, I was growing through it all; how marvelous. On top of all that, the Lord was giving me songs and sermons to write.

For comfort, I encourage you to write out prayers as I did from Colossians. Let me give you an example: Get a notebook, read Colossians 1:9. Rewrite it something like this. Lord, **I** desire to be filled with the knowledge of Your will in all wisdom and spiritual understanding. Lord, **I** want to walk worthy of You unto all pleasing, being fruitful in every good work, and increasing in the knowledge of Thee. Strengthen **me** with all of Your might, according to Your glorious power, unto all patience and longsuffering with joyfulness, in Jesus' name. Colossians 3:8 – Lord, help **me** to put off anger, wrath, malice, blasphemy and filthy communication out of **my** mouth; verse 12 – Lord help **me** put on bowels of mercy, kindness, humbleness of mind, meekness, longsuffering and forbearance. Lord, help **me** to forgive as You forgave **me**. Help **me** to put on charity; let Your peace rule in **my** heart. I desire a heart of thanksgiving. Let Your Word dwell in **me** richly in all wisdom. I desire to teach others and admonish others in psalms, hymns and spiritual songs, singing with grace in **my** heart to You O' God.

Bring the tablet to your prayer room. During your next prayer time, read the prayers that you wrote on yesterday aloud first, and then pray as you usually do, then write new personal prayers from the scriptures. Each day there should be more prayers to pray. Once you fill the notebook up with prayers, date it and start a new book. Who knows, those notebooks may become your published prayer book. You should never run out of words to pray when you pray from the Word.

I had already begun praying in tongues on a daily basis, thanks to my niece, Tiny. Remember the 12 year old who spoke in tongues in my car, causing the Lord to prevent me from driving over my husband. Well, years later, I desired to have those tongues. I knew that there was power in speaking in tongues. I wanted that power. If the Lord could stop a car, just by a little girl speaking in tongues, I was curious as to what else He could stop or block. I wanted to know. I learned that when we speak in tongues, we speak not unto men but mysteries unto the Lord, I Corinthians 14:2.

Anyway, the written prayers were additional prayer techniques the Lord gave me. When I learned about 5:00 a.m. prayer held at a church near my home, which happens to be my current church, I attended daily. It was peaceful there; I wanted to take advantage of the serenity, so I prayed at home and went there to hear from the Lord. I brought my notebook and the Lord spoke to me. The lights were dim and it was a true blessing. I received great revelation on how to handle situations, the church members, my kids and Claxton.

My desire to see more from God was greater. I wanted more visitations, more visions, more dreams, more words from the Lord, and more songs. I wanted to know how other pastors lived outside of the church, so I asked the Lord and He answered. When I visited churches or when we had visiting ministers, the Lord showed me something that only He could. As preachers stood to the podium to preach, the podium turned into a thermometer. The podium turned red. It turned either totally red, partially red, or not at all. The Lord told me that the red represented how much time the preachers spent with Him. When the podium was not red, that meant that the preacher spent no time with Jesus; he was empty. When it was fully red, the preacher was full; fully fasted up, fully prayed up, and fully studied up. What does a pastor's wife do when it is made known to her by the Lord that the preacher is empty? Allow me to answer. She does nothing because she is obligated, like I was, to stay and suffer through the sermon, especially if it is a pastor's anniversary service, revival or a visiting preacher in her home church. The next time you're at an anniversary service and all of the Pastor's wives are clustered in a designated area being individually or corporately envied by her haters, and the speaker is dry, if you are prayed up and are revealed the same, you can go home if you choose to. Do me a favor, in route home, pray for the Pastor's wives who are stuck, trapped or shackled to her seat forced to listen to a preacher on empty. She cannot leave. She has to subject her spirit to inhale junk. It's almost like inhaling secondhand smoke.

Here's another revelation I received in that powerful church. The Lord told me that as people entered Greater Power Pentecostal's front doors, a spirit hovered above the doorways, resting upon the visitors. This spirit's purpose was to pin the visitors down to their seats so that they would not move to the altar during altar call. This spirit also rested upon the visitors so that they were distracted during the sermon; and the spirit kept them from returning to the church. That was a strong demon. I was responsible for calling the visitors; thanking them for coming to visit us. Many of them wanted to talk to me and have prayer with me, but couldn't come back to the church. The revelation the Lord gave me helped me to strategize my prayers. There was also a spirit about two years later that hovered in the front of the three aisles, right at the front pew. When souls went to the altar, this unclean spirit rested upon them heavily. As they returned to their seats, the souls received a second splash of this unclean spirit so that when they sat down, they were heavier laden than they were prior to getting up. We started getting reports about the heaviness in the church from visitors and speakers. Note that the altar workers were not fasting and praying either, so when spirits transferred, they were also heavier going home than they were when they came to church. I had so much information and revelation and no one to share it with. Claxton couldn't see what I saw; therefore, he couldn't hear, believe or understand the revelation I received. Don't forget, I didn't have a degree and without a degree in Claxton's eyes, I wasn't educated enough to hear from the Lord. After all, everyone in the Bible was degreed.

One day, I prayed, asking the Lord to allow the saints to witness something they'd never seen or experienced before. On a Sunday, I went to the altar for prayer; I was the last one to go up. You know how someone stands behind you at the altar? I felt someone's hand on my back as I was praying and getting prayed for. I could hear the uproar of the people from afar. When I sat down, my friend said, "You started all this, let me get me some." She started rubbing my back. What I learned was that different people were coming to the altar just to touch my back. I thought that it was just one person the entire time. When they touched it, they danced, hollered, worshipped, fell or something. The entire church was affected for about 30-45 minutes. Glory swept through the sanctuary though I didn't understand Glory then like I do now due to my current pastor, Bishop Larry Baylor.

I told the Lord in prayer that I wanted to witness the manifestations of Him because I was tired of witnessing the manifestations of the devil. I believed that miracles were taking place in other countries and I wanted to know about them. He answers every time. I saw a seasoned man in the grocery store, trying to get an item off of the shelf. I assisted him, he thanked me and we began to talk about the Lord. He said that he had something to give to me, so we met the next day in a public place. It was a tape entitled Transformations. When I got home and viewed it, I saw miracles from all over the world from people who fasted and prayed. He had no idea of my requests made unto the Lord. When we desire more from the Lord and ask Him for it, expect it. Also, the Lord used the need of a man, knowing the compassion I have for seniors, to connect me with what I inquired about and desired; the manifestations of Him.

I had my last child at a very old age I thought; thirty-six. I was struggling with this little girl that Claxton was dying to have. I needed help and couldn't get adjusted with the chair, the car seat, the bottles, the Pampers, the time with her or the well-baby care. I prayed for help with her and a lady from the church called me about three weeks later telling me, not asking me, that she was picking my baby up every Friday and bringing her to church on Sunday. What a blessing! This really happened. Not only on the weekends, but for holidays she'd take my baby down south to be with her family. I was free every weekend for a long time. This is what prayer does.

In 2009, I fasted every Monday, Wednesday and Friday, eating nothing from 6:00 a.m. until 6:00 a.m. the next morning beginning in February. The sole purpose was for miracles, signs and wonders. I wanted to see angels walk past me. I wanted folk to be healed as they walked in my shadow like Peter. I wanted more visitations from the Lord Himself. I wanted to smile at people and witness inner healing. I wanted walls to literally shake as I prayed. I wanted storms to cease at my voice. I wanted to walk through the hospitals, going on every floor, passing rooms, witnessing every person's healing. I wanted to hear the thoughts of people and so much more. I continued this fast until July. I then went on a 21-day Daniel fast from the first to the twenty-first. While on that fast, the Lord told me to go back to the Monday, Wednesday, and Friday fast. In the midst of all of that, my son was due to come home from out of town to help me with my chocolate chip cookie company. I hadn't heard from him and was wondering where he was. I asked the Lord to show me where he was. The Lord said to Google him. I brushed that off because I knew that that wasn't the Lord speaking. I had a vision that my son was shot by a police officer and in the vision I felt the bullet. It was like I stood behind him and took the shot in my back. I shook myself out of that vision into a powerful prayer. I believe that my prayer was that blocker. A few more weeks had passed and I asked the Lord again. He said to Google him. I said, "Lord, You told me that a few weeks ago." I Googled him and there he was. I couldn't believe it, my child was in jail. The picture of him was not small and dim. It was in live and living color, covering my screen. My heart was pumping so fast I thought I was going to check out of here. I always told my boys not to call me should they ever get locked up because I didn't have money for an attorney and I wasn't putting up my house for them to get out. Guess what? He did not call me. Please don't ever tell your kids that. When we finally connected, I sent him material to read, including my books. I asked the Lord to speak to him while he was still. I reminded the Lord that my son knew His voice and could feel his presence. He was facing 15 years for strong-armed robbery. The court date finally came. He called me afterward to inform me that he was still facing 15 years and that there was nothing the attorney could do. This was on a Friday evening. When I heard those words coming from my son; my saved, sanctified and Holy Ghost filled son; I was at stroke state. I hung up the phone and began to talk to He who could do all things; He who could be my judge and attorney, not just outside of the courtroom, but outside of the state; He who could hear me in a whisper. I said, "Lord, work a miracle for me. I have been fasting since February, specifically for miracles, signs, and wonders. Release him like you did Peter. Peter had four sets of four guards guarding him and You released him and set him free. Set my son free like you did Peter." My heart was aching. I didn't have empathy for the young people who were incarcerated, but I did pray comforting prayers for their parents though I couldn't feel their hurt. Somebody say, "On Tuesday." The guard interrupted my son's game that he was viewing on the television and said, "You are being released." He was taken over to the other side of town so that he could be set free in the morning. When morning came, he was set free, meaning that he had no felony. Ain't the Lord all right? Just as I prayed, "Release him and set him free." When my son came home I asked him about my vision I had about him running from the police. He said that it did happen, but he was shot with a taser gun. The cop could have been planning to use the real gun or maybe the devil told the cop that my son was armed. I believe that my prayer changed his mind to use the taser gun. In the vision when I stood behind him to block the bullet, I believe that the prayer I prayed was the blocker.

I wish I could testify that my son is beating the deacon to the church on Sunday's to get a seat. I guess I'll have to go back to my three-days-a-week fast. He did complete cooking school and he is employed.

The church I attend now is a fasting church where miracles, signs and wonders are happening. I asked the Lord to cause my fingertips to become red hot so that I will know when to lay hands on people for healing without doubt. One Wednesday, during dismissal of our afternoon Bible class, our pastor was praying. I noticed that my fingertips were scorching hot. I said to myself, "The Lord heard me, wow!" At the same time the pastor stopped praying the dismissal prayer and said, "I feel led of the Lord to do this. Sister Morgan, come help me pray for the sister here. Sister Morgan is one of the First Ladies here at our church and…" He went on to tell the people who I was. He asked me to lay my hands on her chest and he laid his hands on top of mine. The lady was healed of lung cancer. The following week, the same thing happened. The lady said that the doctors couldn't find the cancer in her lungs, but they diagnosed her with cancer in another area. The heat came over my fingers again, the pastor called me up to assist him and she was healed.

I encourage you to increase your prayer life; wait on the Lord, listen to His voice; move when He says move and write down what He says.

Chapter 5

Pastor's wives

Claxton resigned as pastor of Greater Power Pentecostal in 2007. He moved back home the following January and started a healing ministry which lasted six weeks. What lasted six weeks? I can answer that; the move home and the ministry. He wasn't ready yet, though he said, "The Lord said." After attending one church for over 40 years and no longer being there, he needed healing.

Claxton stopped coming to the church. He couldn't get out of bed. I opened the services, I was the praise and worship leader, I conducted the services, I brought the messages, I took up the tithes and offering, I gave the altar call, I made the announcements, I dismissed, I paid the rent, and I made the deposits. I said to myself, "Now wait just a minute here, I ain't no pastor. How did this happen?" When I came to myself, I shut that church down because I was not called to pastor. Guess who was one of the members? You've guessed it, Airika. I was wondering how the ministry was going to be blessed when it opened with curses attached? I'm not denying the Lord's Words to Claxton concerning the ministry. I believe that the timing was for later.

I am so thankful unto God for teaching me how to walk in the spirit of humility and the importance of it. Had the Lord not taught me this, I believe my mind would have snapped some time during my 10-year training ground as a pastor's wife. So many Pastor's wives walk in the spirit of pride whereas they become non-teachable, non-approachable and non-coachable. It's a blessing to always be in the position to learn, assist and submit. We take the scripture out of context when we say, "I'm the head and not the tail, above and not beneath." As heads, this means that we are the head as in operating in greatness because Jesus is great, the Great I AM and having the mind of Christ. The tail represents walking in darkness. Above means to follow Jesus; walking in holiness. He is the Most High God, so we are looking up to Him. We are lifting up our eyes unto Him and lifting up our heads; and thinking on things which are above. What beneath means is foolishness, worldliness, unrighteousness. For some reason, folk with titles (especially Pastor's wives) think that being the head means they're greater than others and being above means that others must look up to them as in worshipping them; how carnal. Beneath to them means that people are below them as in meaningless or unworthy.

Pastor's wives, God placed us in the position to assist our husbands with training and directing sheep, preparing them for their eternal destination.

When our focus is on everything other than that, we need to consult God; we're missing it. Men and women of God deserve nice material possessions and they should be financially solvent. This way, they can focus on the things of the Lord and not be distracted by debt. When we get "my seat" versus "the judgment seat" or "my garments" versus "the garments of praise" or "my nails and feet" versus "the nails in Jesus' feet" or "my head" versus "the head" confused with what's first on the Kingdom agenda, we're in trouble.

Pastor's wives, as the lead women in your church, you cannot afford to have picks and chooses. Every woman is special and needs your assistance in some way. Don't cause her to leave the ministry due to your behavior. The visitor's report should not be that the pastor's wife is running the church or the pastor's wife won't sit down.

It is known that every person will not be loved or liked, but as a pastor's wife, you have to love at all times. Even when people hurt you, you have to pray for them and let the Lord fight your battles for you. I hear you saying, "I am not where you are yet or I am not there." I see some of your necks rolling, but the bottom line is, are we going to stand on the Word or not?

When we are witnessing or counseling, it is irrelevant to share our title; this does not justify our righteousness with Jesus. When witnessing to relatives, please don't act as if you were always holy. Remember, they remember our history. Please don't act as if you are greater than the people you're speaking with. When we're speaking with teenagers, we must keep it real. Allow the Lord to tell you which testimonies to share. Let me share a witnessing secret with you. Humble yourself! Make the listeners feel

as if they are special and mean a lot to you. Display sincere
compassion and believe me, warm hearts are felt. Come
down to their level temporarily so that trust is developed.
When you are trusted, they are free to open up to share.
Once this happens, then you can minister. When it is
learned later that you are the pastor's wife, you will be
appreciated and respected more. When they know that you
are really concerned about their soul, it is unforgettable.
We have to remember that we are nothing without God and
we have to make others feel as if they are someone in the
eyes of God.

Every year I looked forward to attending our national
conventions which were held in various states. I registered
with the ministers' wives ministry so that I could grasp
new concepts to take back to my church for myself and
for our ministers' wives. I was wrestling with issues that
were not up for discussion like jealousy, envy, lying, lust,
hatred, fornication, deception, adultery, and everything that
you can think of. When I got to the seminars, the subjects
were on health issues, weight loss, cooking, exercising,
housekeeping, raising our children, and church services,
which were good. I was frustrated after every seminar,
luncheon and banquet. I couldn't believe that no one
spoke or taught on subjects for me. I was thinking that
maybe I was the only one in this kind of trouble. While in
attendance of the meetings, I listened to the ladies laugh
and holler out at what was said by the speakers and I felt
like hiding under the chair. I did not want anyone to know
that I was in trouble or that I was troubled. I couldn't share

my issues with anyone sitting close to me; I didn't know them. As I listened, I was thinking that my marriage was the only one that was shaky. Then, I'd ask myself, "Are all their ministries trouble-free?" I was puzzled. Prior to every seminar I'd say to myself, "Maybe this one will help me." At the end of the convention, I was ready; ready to run and never to return home. I was heavier going back home from the convention than I was coming. There was no teaching for me, no prayer and no deliverance; for years. Had somebody asked, "Did anybody come here bound? Let me pray for you." I would have crawled to the front. Everybody looked pretty; everybody looked saved; and everybody looked free. They say, "Looks are deceiving." I must commend "They."

Pastor's wives, do me a favor. If you are in the position to get a message to headquarters of your national or international convention, conference, or convocation, the ministers' wives department, please tell them that Lady Bea said to allot some time during the seminars to teach on the demonic. Suggest that time is permitted for the Pastor's wives to pray so that healing and deliverance can take place. Suggest teachings on handling the husband who do not love his wife as Jesus loves the church. Suggest teachings on the spirit of Jezebel within the church and how to deal with it. Prior to our convention, the choir leaders sent out choir attire letters to the choir members for uniformity purposes; how awesome. If the ministers' wives prepare for the convention with prayer and fasting schedules, similar to the choir attire notices, I believe that transformation will take place during the sessions. When they return home, they will be excited to utilize the teachings and witnessing the Lord's work. No pastor's wife should feel like I felt after a convention. All of the deep prayer warriors, all of the prophetesses, all who possessed the gifts of the spirit, and most of all, all of the Holy Ghost power that was supposed to had been there, but yet, I was not set free. It was kind of like going to Six Flags. You're excited about going; you're looking forward to it. You plan for it! You purchase your tickets, of course looking for coupons or discounts; then pack your cooler. You're having a good time in route there. You arrive, you see people that you know. You start taking pictures; then, race to get to your favorite roller coaster, you know how we do? You stand in a long line. Finally, it's your turn to sit in the seat of the ride. You secure your personal effects, fasten up, and smiling; ready to scream. Then, you take off slowly, going around curves from the left to the right. Then, slowly climb to the top of the hill, many feet up, anticipating the fast downward slope, which is the most exciting part of the ride. Here you are sitting at the top, waiting, and the ride malfunctions. Now, you're frustrated. No need to complain, the ride is being repaired. All of the other riders aren't saying anything either, but they are just as frustrated. After the ride is all over, you get off and you're tired, neck and back are hurting; ready to go home; wished you had not come and feeling like you've wasted time, money and energy. The analogy is a bit extreme, but I pray that it brought clarity to my point. When we attend conventions, convocations, or conferences, we must expect changes.

Otherwise, we're just meeting. In that case, we can meet up on Skype.

I must give the Lord credit for keeping my mind on Him. Sometimes, as we go through our struggles, Satan will drop a thought upon us to do evil. As you know, a thought is his only entrance. I call that thought a seed. We have the power to water the seed of Satan by acting on it, sharing it, or meditating on it. Or, we can use our power to kill the seed by praying the scriptures, example: Knowing that whatsoever good thing any man doeth, the same shall he receive of the Lord, whether he be bond or free, Ephesians 5:8 or, But he that doeth wrong shall receive for the wrong which he hath done, Colossians 3:2. Scriptures are deterrents from sin. They serve as astringents, cleansing our thoughts; purifying our mind. We can also plead the blood of Jesus when trouble is upon us or when temptation is facing us by saying, "The blood of Jesus is against you Satan or I plead the blood of Jesus for there is power in it." As Jesus was beaten for the sins that we committed, He shed blood. His blood was shed so that our sins could be forgiven. Because His blood was shed, it protects us from sinning and from eternal death; we shall have eternal life, 1 John 5:11. The blood also protects us when we are attacked as it was in Exodus 12:1-14. We can kill unclean thoughts when we plead His blood. We can also kill unclean thoughts by casting down imaginations, II Corinthians 2:5. We can pray saying, "Satan, I cast this (say the thought aloud) out of my mind, in the name of Jesus. These are the measures I had to take to keep from doing evil. Satan spoke to me often. He'd tell me to expose personal information of the members. He'd tell me to slash tires, burst windows, and to hit some of the people upside their head. The Lord spoke to me, reminded me of the consequences of my wrongdoing. The scriptures would cleanse my thoughts and then I'd repent. Though I knew that the Lord would fight my battles, sometimes I wanted to handle my matters my way. I always ended up giving in and doing it God's way. Through my years of suffering, I continued to cook and clean for my husband with great joy and I referenced him as the Bible commands. One thing Claxton can say is that I was always kind to him, soft-spoken, understanding, and continuously walked in the spirit of forgiveness, even during heated discussions. Claxton used to tell me that he wished he was more like me by not allowing my troubles to overtake me. He that hath no rule over his own spirit is like a city that is broken down, and without walls, Proverbs 25:28. A city that is broken down without walls has no rules, no laws, no boundaries, no limits, or no order; therefore, anything goes. When our spirit is like the city without walls, we'll say or do anything our way. We want to say and do what thus saith the Lord. Whatever we do, we must remember that we are doing it as unto the Lord. This way, we will enjoy it regardless to what's happening to us or what's being said about us. We're pleasing the Lord.

Chapter 6

The Absence of Dads in Ministry

- In 2004, my son, Pooky, kept running away. He'd disappear after school and his reason was he didn't want to live at home. The school was calling me often. They always wanted to suspend him because he knew who fought, who caused the fights and who the bullies were. I was tired of meeting with the counselor and principal. Claxton was hardly home and when he was, he had no time for these issues. Pooky was the youngest son and he was really young when we married. Therefore, he didn't get whippings as the others did; he was the baby. I was always looking for him after school; he kept me off focus. I found myself worrying about him and I am not a worrier. It became too much; it was overwhelming. It crept up on me. I don't let situations get the best of me, but this one did. I decided to cast this care upon the Lord for He careth for me. I said, "I am not worrying with Pooky anymore, whatever happens, happens and it won't be my worry, it will be the Lord's. I turned it over to Jesus." I was on the phone, sharing this with my friend, Jacie. As soon as we hung up the phone, the phone rang. I thought she was calling me right back; it was the school's nurse telling me Pooky fell and was paralyzed from the waist down. I was tested again. My faith was tried. They called the ambulance. I did not panic. I said to the Lord, "You are my Healer; Pooky is in your hands. If You can't do it, it can't get done. This is Your child." When I arrived at the school, the nurse, counselor, and principal were shaken up and out of breath. There my son was, lying on the stretcher, he couldn't move. I kissed him and whispered in his ear that he was going to be all right. When we got to the hospital, they ran many tests. I was reading my Bible as we waited for the results. We were there for hours. Then, as I was reading Revelation, Chapter 5, the Lord gave me the melody of a new song from verse 12. As I began singing, power came into the room and I saw Pooky's foot move. I kept singing, he kept moving and I kept singing. Then he said he needed to use the restroom. I said, "What are you going to do?" He wanted me to hold the urinal. I said, "Boy, if I'm holding the urinal, what will you be doing? I'm not holding that or that." He laughed so hard. The hospital staff assisted him. I had not realized Pooky was healed. When it hit me, I said, "Let's go." I never saw the results of the tests, never saw the doctors, I never got a bill and Pooky never ran away again. Satan will use anybody to distract us. Claxton never called or came to check on Pooky.

- When Claxton left home, my other son started sneaking out of the house and climbing back in through his bedroom window. One midnight, I heard this noise coming from one of the bedrooms. I checked and what do you think I rolled up on? I went in his room, flipped on the light and there he was. He was coming through the window. His feet were still hanging out of the window and arms extended forward. I crossed my arms across my chest, we looked at each other and I said, "So you're Superman?" He was shaking and said, "No." I said, "You're flying through windows. Where are you coming from?" He said, "Walking." I said, "Walking? At midnight? On a school night? You look like you've been flying." Of course, he moved out. My rules were too great for him. He lived in about 12 homes of his friends before moving to another state with his best friend. He enrolled himself into high school and graduated.

- Absent, but yet residing with your children, is hard on the children. That's worst than being absent from the home and their lives. Take them with you sometimes. Take them to the church and train them. Claxton was responsible for four sons and I suggested to him to train each one to master one ministry and train all of them to be his armor bearer; he couldn't hear me.

- Pastors, husbands and leaders, please don't let the ministry interrupt family life. Ask the Lord to help you balance ministry, family and employment if you're still employed. Don't miss all of the sporting events, school conferences, and field trips with your kids. Plan family nights and vacations. Men, if your children become accustomed to your absenteeism, your presence will irritate them when you do decide to stay home. Don't be a stranger to your family. I told Claxton to keep God first in his life, then his family, then the church because if he no longer pastors, he'd still have God and his family. But he placed the church first and now he has nothing.

Chapter 7

Bound Pastor's wives

Pastor's wives, I know some of you are bound and no one knows about it. I learned that bondage falls into different categories. A few of them are:

a. Some Pastor's wives are bound at home and at church. Their husbands are jealous and envious of them and blocking them from going forward in ministry.

b. Some Pastor's wives appear to be free while at church, but suffering at home. They look nice, dress nice, hair and nails are always on point, drives nice cars, living in prestigious neighborhoods, but yet, miserable.

c. Some Pastor's wives are free in their home and free with their husband, but when they get to the church, haters are lined up at the door. This is a case that can be easily handled because her husband has her back; he is on her side. They can work together, casting out unclean spirits. The world can come against her; it doesn't matter when her husband is with her.

d. Some Pastor's wives suffer due to personal spiritual weaknesses. They possess unclean spirits such as unforgiveness, hatred, jealousy, envy, control, low self-esteem, selfishness, anger, untreated depression to name a few. Her husband loves her; the church members love her, but she is yoked; she is bound; and she is spiritually blind. She can't see what God has before her. She cannot see because she is bound.

e. Some Pastor's wives are truly free at church and at home. They are free to voice their opinion and suggestions. If a sister is out of line, they are free to correct her. They are also free to error, free to operate in spiritual gifts, free to minister, free of worry and fear. They are free to plan functions without permission; only having to inform spouse. They are free in Jesus with peace in the home and genuine love in the marriage. If this is you, you are to be the head of fasting and praying committees for all women, especially Pastor's wives.

I know it gets lonely at the top, top, as in being the pastor's wife. Your husband is always absent from the home. He is forever in a meeting, performing weddings and funerals, visiting the sick and shut in, studying, counseling and praying. You feel like a single parent. You're the only one disciplining the children, shopping, helping with homework, sports, parent/teacher conferences, handling the chores and the checkbook. Know that I am praying for you; I know it's not easy.

No one can believe that the pastor's wife is abused, but she is. You haven't heard? Who can she tell? Can she trust you? Oh, you asked, "Where are the bruises?"

THE UNSEEN ABUSE

MENTAL ABUSE – When a person says something or does something that affects your thinking. Example: My husband used to tell me how ugly I was. Every time I got dressed, I felt ugly. No matter how my hair looked or how well my suit fit, I remembered what he said, "With your old, ugly self." Also, mental abuse is when you are blamed for the mistakes of others, blamed for incomplete tasks, and makes you think that what you do, no matter how it's done, is wrong. Mental abuse is when your husband considers everything you do is small, unimportant or irrelevant. He calls your wisdom foolish and your sweetness bitter. Regardless to your education or experiences, to him you're dumb, ignorant, stupid or crazy. This abuse causes the abuser's words to repeat themselves in your head and lasts long periods of time, sometimes years. The abuser can make you think what they want you to think as if you have no mind. For them to admit you're right really means they're admitting that they're wrong which is not happening unless God intervenes.

EMOTIONAL ABUSE – When a person is threatened. Example: If you do or say this, then I will make sure I do this to you. This causes a person to live in fear and it makes you feel unworthy, sad and small. Humiliation is emotional abuse. Claxton used to get all his sisters greeting cards, call them up to the pulpit and present them with money attached. He'd give me my card at home (empty) and knew I didn't have money. He'd announce, "First

Lady received her card at home." That's humiliation. Embarrassment is another form. When my family came over on holidays, Claxton would stay in the bedroom or in his office, and then leave without eating, learning later from other people that he ate at some of the sisters' homes. Not communicating is another form of emotional abuse. How do you walk into your own home and not speak to your own family. Okay, you're mad. What does that have to do with saying, "Hi?" How long does it take to say, "Hi?" How can you shut down from your family for weeks? How can you be away from your family and not check on them and won't answer your telephone? How can you ignore your wife as she speaks or ignore your wife's needs? How can you eat a meal away from home, wipe your mouth, rub your full stomach, belch, and not know whether or not your family has eaten? How can you distribute money to women in need and your wife is in need. How do you have a comforting word for other women, but your wife is in dire need of your kindness? How do you hang up the telephone on your wife? How can you not try to get an understanding of a situation from your wife? How do you walk out of a room or house without listening to your wife? These are some of the issues I personally endured. Oh, I didn't mention control. Being in control is being the head of your home, being directed by the Lord. Being controlling is following the direction of Satan in decision making. A controller exemplifies the power of man. The husband in control of a home exemplifies the power of Jesus. Another form of emotional abuse is when your spouse is unaffectionate, moody, and has an ugly voice tone whenever he does decide to speak to you.

Every incident above was experienced by me. I could not share this information as a pastor's wife; I was bound. We were taught back in the day not to discuss anything that goes on in the home. Pastor's wives, you have to release your troubles in prayer first; you need a prayer partner. You need a fasting partner; you need a confidant. You have to be led by the Lord as to who to talk to though. Remember, when you confide in other Pastor's wives, they share with their husbands and when the pastors meet, it is discussed. I had an awesome opportunity to speak with a seasoned pastor's wife when I was a new pastor's wife. She told me to get a friend outside of the church to share my church troubles with. She said if I hold all of that stuff in, it will kill me. This was the late First Lady Josephine Johnson. I'm passing it on to you. Make sure you hear from the Lord as to who to tell what to. When you hear from Him, take heed.

Ask the Lord to show you how to separate your husband from your pastor so you won't come to church mad at the world. Deal with your husband at home; handle your pastor at church. Whatever you do at church that is considered negative, the saints will remember it forever. For some reason, they don't remember the good. If women are acting a fool with your husband at church, don't sweat it. Address it with your husband at home. Put Jesus on them and watch God move. I have witnessed the move of

God on people I placed in His hands. The Lord will fight your battles for you just as He did for king Jehoshaphat.

There are other forms of abuse such as spiritual, verbal, financial and physical. Two or three forms can easily be displayed in one act. I experienced them all, except physical.

Pastor's wives, you can be free today. Call a fast, don't wait on the pastor to call one, you do it. You can be free in your spirit through fasting and praying. I am by no means advocating family division. If you desire freedom as in divorce, that's out of my jurisdiction, but do seek counseling.

Chapter 8

The Modern Day Moses, Aaron and Hur

Each Leader is considered a "Moses" of their ministry.

In Exodus, Chapter 17, Moses, who led the Israelites, instructed Joshua to select men to fight the Amalekites on the field while Moses fought in prayer. The leaders are the prayer warriors.

The Bible says during this war, Moses got weary; he was losing strength to carry on. Leaders sometimes get weary.

The Bible says Moses climbed to the top of the mountain and he could oversee the war. When he lifted his hands, his men were winning the fight or prevailing. But when he lowered his hands, the enemy, the Amalekites were winning or prevailing.

Sometimes leaders don't feel like lifting their hands in prayer; they get tired, just like Moses did.

The Bible says Aaron and Hur placed a rock under Moses so he could rest. Aaron lifted one of Moses' hands as Hur lifted his other hand. With this excellent assistance, the Israelites prevailed. Leaders desire to prevail. When they get tired, they need some Aarons and some Hurs to keep their hands lifted.

Leaders, we need to be the Aarons and the Hurs for each other.

Moses rested upon "a" rock; we have to rest upon "the" Rock which is Jesus Christ. He is the Rock, his work is perfect: for all his ways are judgment: a God of truth and without iniquity, just and right is he, *Deuteronomy 32:4.*

There is none holy as the LORD: for there is none beside thee: neither is there any rock like our God, *I Samuel 2:2.*

Moses instructed Joshua to select men to fight on the field while he fought in prayer. This means the pastor should delegate someone to form a prayer team or the leader of a group should delegate someone to form a prayer team. The pastors need Aarons and Hurs to personally assist him, so does the pastor's wife, along with all of the leaders.

Leaders, do me a favor. Form a committee, consisting of a group of leaders of the same title or position as you. Each leader will labor in prayer and fasting for all of the other leaders. Instead of you focusing on your situations, your focus will be on other leaders' situations. You will be prayer warriors one to another. Do this on a regular basis. It doesn't matter the education, status or age. When it all boils down, when we're hurting, we are of the same creed and gender. Do you know how powerful this would be if a group of pastors fasted and prayed together or a group of policemen or school teachers? How about a group of governors or senators? I can see cities coming together in fasting and prayer. I see states coming together in fasting and prayer. I see each city divided by municipalities to fast and pray together. Satan strategically plans attacks and he is successful. We have to outthink him. We're so busy trying to outdo, outthink and outsmart each other and our neighbor, not realizing it's all in Satan's plan. We need to come together to double team him. We plan baby showers, bridal showers, housewarmings, bachelor parties, and Super Bowl gatherings with most attendees eating and not interested in the game. What if we planned a Fasting Prep Party? Send out invitations just like we usually do (Facebook, hand bills, telephone tree, Website). As guests arrive, list their names in a notebook. You know refreshments draw crowds, especially after church! Please don't serve heavy food because my niece told me it is easy for her to commit to fasting when she is stuffed. So, serve light refreshments. As we discuss the greatest issues of the church or family, we'll write them down. Then we'll narrow each issue down to one word, then write down the spirit that the issue carries, placing it directly next to the issue. Example: Sister Jelly is not totally honest; we'll write her name down and the unclean spirit next to it, which is lying (call it what it is) because the truth is the light. This way, we'll know what spirits we're working with which gives us the purpose of the first fast; decide together what to abstain from; create two fasting options to consider those taking medication; discuss prayer schedules so prayer can take place around the clock or in shifts (9, 12, 3, 6) or have prayer service on the "free" telephone conference calling system. Decide the length, starting date, ending date, and times for the fast. If we partake in the Daniel Fast outlined in this book, the length of the fast is already set, 10 days. Then we'll appoint a record keeper to be the recipient of all testimonies. We'll appoint one person to make calls to check on each faster's progress or form a prayer chain where the leader calls the first person on the list to check on them and to have prayer with them. Then the first person on the list calls the second person to check on them and to have prayer as well and so on. The last person on the list calls the leader. However it's done, pray one for another, encourage each other, conduct your own private praise and worship services in your car or home, thank the Lord now for what's about to happen and witness God's hand move.

Let's say the group of leaders who are fasting and praying are Pastor's wives. When the pastor's wife is strengthened, encouraged, comforted, delivered (set free), and healed, she will be equipped to minister to the wives within her church; the deacon's wife, the minister's wife, the musician's wife, the usher's wife, the policeman's wife, the pilot's wife, the mayor's wife, the governor's wife, the firefighter's wife, the principal's wife, all other wives and all aspiring wives.

Also, not only will the pastor's wife be better equipped to minister to the women within her church, she will be better equipped to minister to her own husband, encouraging him. When the pastor is encouraged, enlightened, and uplifted, what a greater work he will do for the Lord within the congregation. The wives of the church will be equipped to minister to their spouses as well.

We're waiting for you Moses, Aaron and Hur!

Chapter 9

Lay Members

Usually, after walking in the imagination of our own heart, living according to our own will and ready to live in holiness, we join a church, then join the choir or usher board and we think we're safe.

As new lay members or new saints, we have responsibilities that are not always taught to us by the church officials. We've learned them by trial and error over the years. Some of us don't know what to expect once we join a church. Some of us may have been out of church for years and now that we're back in, we have either forgotten church etiquette or never knew they existed. There are guidelines for us to follow suitable for all denominations.

Let me share some do's and don'ts of ministry:

- If the church offers new saints' or new members' classes, sign up, attend and read the books and pamphlets. Some churches' classes are mandatory. Though you may be a member who has transferred from another church and may have been in church for years, this has nothing to do with the rules and regulations of this church. Unless the pastor excuses you from the class, you are expected to attend the course.

- Find out about the dress code of the church. Though we are to come to church as we are, this does not mean we are to stay as we are. We had single female members attending our church in club clothes every Sunday; grew up in the church and knew better. Besides, the Lord will speak to us letting us know when we are inappropriately dressed; we just ignore it. When we are dressed to grasp the attention of men at church, we don't realize that it is a distraction to many though this may be your motive. Let me share this, when we interfere with God's work, rather it's being the distraction to the sermon, the praying, the singing, the praising, or the worship, there are consequences. God is angry.

- Learn the necessary channels to reach the pastor. Find out whether or not you go through his wife first or if you meet with them both or if you're to set an appointment through the secretary. Our home phone was used to transact church business in the early stages of the ministry. When the saints lied on me, saying they had left many messages with me, insinuating that I was not relaying messages to Claxton, he believed them. From then on, he could be reached on his cell phone, personal office phone at home or on the church office phone. He was the only one retrieving messages. By him informing the congregation that it was okay to leave messages for him because no one else listened to them, what kind of messages do you think were left by silly carnal sisters?

- Please don't bombard the pastor with all of your issues every Sunday after church, remember that pastor studied all week, prayed, met with people, prepared messages and lessons, preached and taught, conducted service, and greeted the saints and visitors. The pastor is tired and hungry. Not to mention two or more services may have been conducted. I remember one of the saints had to meet Claxton after every Sunday service, after every Bible class and after every prayer meeting, every week. For what? She was not his only member and he surely wasn't God! You know when you're meeting with the pastor too often; after every service is too often. When you're spending time with the pastor, consider the fact that he could be utilizing that same time with his family so don't waste his time with foolishness. If you're out eating with the pastor regularly and his wife is absent, what are your thoughts about it? Claxton was eating out all of the time in my absence. I didn't learn about it from him until I confronted him. Other church members called to tell me. Remember, I cooked big dinners.

- Before meeting with the pastor, concerning your issues, make sure you have prayed, fasted and meditated about it first. Give the Lord an opportunity to answer your petitions. After you've done all you've known to do, then seek counsel from your pastor. Your pastor will teach you to trust in Your God "first" before solely depending upon him or her. Otherwise, if the pastor passes away or no longer pastors, what happens if all of our trust and faith is in him and not in God?

- Sisters, when you have special gifts for the pastor, please don't ask the deacon to unlock the pastor's office so you can leave them on his desk. You've got to know this happened to me. Remember Willimina? She was Claxton's best friend. When Claxton was installed as Pastor, he didn't get a chance to be called Pastor yet before this girl ran out and bought a nameplate for his desk. She'd have balloons and gifts awaiting him when he entered his office. You know what? I was told that a deacon let her into the office, but thinking back, she may have had a key.

- During the pastor's anniversary service, please don't place a beautiful bouquet of flowers on a table in between the chairs of the pastor and his wife and then, at the end of the program, snatch the bouquet, the very same bouquet, out of the vase, presenting them to someone else, stating in the microphone that the flowers were never intended for the pastor's wife. That is not the spirit of excellence. This really happened to me!

- When you meet with the pastor, remember he is neither your gynecologist, chiropractor or massage therapist. The pastor has no need to know your inadequacies and deficiencies in the bedroom. If you are single, you ain't got no business telling the pastor your bedroom issues because you shouldn't have any. Just in case there is a typo in your Bible, fornication is sin. You shouldn't be comfortable sharing with the man of God your sin, especially sexual sin knowing you're not seeking advice. I need you to hear this clearly; please do not attempt to entice the pastor. A single woman scheduled a meeting with Claxton and she detailed her sexual troubles, thinking that she was exciting him. What she didn't know was that Claxton was about to regurgitate; that's putting it nicely. What he really said was, "I was about to throw up." This woman was a known witch whose assignment was to bounce from church to church to destroy marriages of pastors and wives. I was warned of the witch before her arrival to our church by one person who had never seen her, then warned that the witch was a member of our church by another person. She only wanted Claxton to pray for her. She was always supposedly slain in the spirit. I used to think to myself, "Get up off of that floor before you get slain for real, quit playing with God." One day during prayer, we were all at the altar, speaking in tongues. Someone was standing behind me, speaking in created tongues. It felt like knives were thrown in my back and hitting me hard. The blows distracted me as I prayed. The Lord said, "Those are not My tongues." I had to leave the altar to see who my attacker was and surely it was the witch. We have to be in tuned with God because He will make known to us spirits that are unlike His. Let me add this. There was another woman who asked Claxton to lay with him and promised him she wouldn't tell anyone about it. Claxton told her he loved his wife and his God too much to do that. Claxton helped lonely, single women; this caused them to feel special and because many were carnal, they believed the doors of the church were open for intimacy. Please don't ask the pastor to lay with you. Isn't the devil ignorant? I helped women on many occasions with clothes for their children, counseling and transportation to places other than church, and much more. These were the ones making propositions with Claxton. Can you believe she said she wouldn't tell anyone? You don't have to broadcast sin. The pregnancy itself would have spoken loudly and clearly, moving across the country faster than e-mail. Don't you know this girl would have been pregnant and collecting child support not to mention bringing the child to church and to my home; kind of like Willimina did with their adopted child? Of course the ministry, the marriage and the members would have been destroyed.

- Right before our wedding, I was sitting in the car waiting for Claxton to come out of the church. It was raining hard. A lady from the church, well-built, dressed in a red outfit, who Claxton knew well, was walking him to the car. She was sharing her umbrella and said to him, "If you try this red out, I promise you will not be getting married next week." Though he wasn't the pastor then, he was the assistant pastor; he was still a man of God. Women, please keep your name good. You shouldn't even want the pastor to think you're trifling. Then, if he tells his wife and she tells her personal friends and they tell their personal friends, do you know how many people that is? We have to consider the consequences for our unrighteousness. We should think ahead asking "what if" questions to ourselves.

- Sometimes, make appointments to meet the pastor to share testimonies rather than your troubles all of the time. Sometimes the pastor wants to know if his messages have been helpful to you or if he has encouraged you. We can encourage the pastor without flirting with him.

- Ask the Lord to give you ways to lighten the load of the pastor, his wife and his family.

- Ask the Lord to teach you how to intercede in prayer for your pastor, his wife and his family. Don't just tell the pastor you're praying for him. What are your prayers? What are you praying?

- Women, if you need a ride to church, call the transportation department first, if one exists, or ask the pastor's wife for a ride if he's married. Women drove our car without my knowledge or approval. Of course my husband was responsible for lending out our car and not communicating with me. It was also the women's responsibility to be respectful to me as a wife and spiritual leader and reverential to our marriage, their pastor, his reputation, his name, his credentials, our church family and most of all, unto the Lord. You've heard the saying, "Never let the devil ride in your car because if you let him ride, he'll want to drive." That's what happened. Claxton picked up women and not just for church and surely those devils were driving the car. Airika was not the only female driving our car, she was the last one.

- Women, please don't prepare and bring your special entrée to the pastor to eat, especially if he has a wife. Save those recipes for your own husband. It's so wonderful you can cook; open a restaurant. If you learn that the pastor's wife can't cook, give her your recipes or direct her to the cooking channel. You're probably saying, "She ain't getting my recipes." Well, don't cook for her husband then. If you really want the pastor to taste your cooking, you would let his wife cook it using your recipe. On many occasions, my husband brought home plates of food and plastic containers of food he received from the sisters at the church. He didn't have the courage to say he didn't want it, so he'd bring that junk home. He didn't eat the food he brought home, but that's not to say he hadn't stuffed himself where he was. Airika said to Claxton in the midst of the saints, "Don't act like you don't eat my cooking because I am still waiting on my plastic bowls to return to their rightful owner." When I heard that I said to myself, "That's what she's going to be doing, waiting." I pitched all of that mess and was waiting on Claxton to clown with me each time, but he never did.

- Ladies, when you see the pastor's wife at church, don't hate on her, love on her. You have no idea what she could be suffering with. If you see her driving a nice car, don't envy her. I drove a Cadillac. I ordered it when they first came out. We got one of the first shipments. You're talking about some attention? Oh, my goodness. I was so excited about that car. It had everything in it. The seat, stereo and mirror settings were programmed to readjust to the key that was in the ignition and what I really liked was the voice recorder on the sun visor. I could record a piece of a song the Lord would give me while in the car. The car was not ordered for me though. This was Claxton's car. I was so excited for him. I had ordered it and he had never heard of it. I like to drive regular cars made for regular people. I love to see others in nice things. I don't like the attention. However, after a year, Claxton no longer wanted that car; he wanted something bigger, the DeVille; so I was stuck with the CTS. This is why I said not to envy others. I didn't have gas money for that car. I was used to putting $10 in my car, driving forever; not with this one. I couldn't afford it. I was always on "E." When I'd pull up somewhere, I could feel the jealousy of my haters, but they just didn't know I barely made it there and had the destination been a mile further, I would have been calling AAA to bring me some gasoline. Later on, Claxton took the car back, which was a blessing, and that was when Airika started driving it. When the saints first saw me behind the wheel of my husband's car, they questioned it. Did you hear me say they questioned me driving my husband's car? There was a crowd around the car. Airika was one of them and I remember her saying, "I'll drive it." And she did. When you see a pastor's wife going to her car, you are going to wonder if she has gas or not. Wonder no more, just hand her a gas card. You do not know her situation. It may not be like mine, I would hope not, but you never know.

- When you are asked to dismiss the service in prayer, remember to pray for the pastor's wife as well as the pastor. So many times during dismissal prayer, I was not mentioned in the prayer and would be right there, holding hands with the one who was praying. Sometimes, after naming everybody's name in the church, including their kids and asking the Lord to bless the pastor, strengthen him, lift him up, bestow wisdom upon him, equip him and enlighten him, then they'd say, "And Lord, and his companion." Not, "And Lord, bless our pastor's wife or bless Sis. Morgan." They'd say, "And his companion" with emphasis on the letter 'p' in companion with a semi-attitude and neck rolling. I used to think to myself, "How far do they think those prayers are going? Certainly not to Heaven."

- When you are concerned about the health of the pastor and you feel led by the Lord to purchase him vitamins remember his wife's health, too. I met a lady who kept her pastor supplied with vitamins. I asked her if she bought his wife's vitamins too and she said, "No, because she does not help him with the ministry." I said, "How do you know she doesn't want to? He may be blocking her from helping him. Maybe he's abusive. Maybe it's all about him." She said she didn't think of it in that sense. Sometimes harm to the pastor's wife is not intentional. Some members are truly sincere about what they do for their pastor and may not have anything against his wife. But then there are others who have corrupt motives. Personally, I purchased some sunflower seeds from Israel for my current pastor. I had been buying them for a while. I've been eating David & Sons, now called David's every day since first grade. In Bible class he mentioned he eats sunflower seeds and he also said in the same class that when we help the people in Israel, how blessed we'd be by God. I was excited about the fact that I was already helping the people by buying the seeds and I knew all proceeds went directly to Israel. In that excitement, the next time I bought me some, I bought the pastor some. I was not thinking about how the pastor's wife may have felt when I did that. It was done in innocence. When I thought about it, long after the fact, I should have mentioned it to her prior to the purchase. I do understand how people can love their pastor and want to do things for him. I didn't have a problem with the members loving their pastor or assisting him. If the women said nothing to me about what they did for Claxton, that was fine. It was when Claxton said nothing to me about what was done and I'd hear about it or overhear about it from others; that was my dilemma.

- Do not compete with the pastor's wife. If you are a better dresser than she is, that's okay. If you purposely try to out-dress her to get the attention of the pastor, you're in dire need of prayer. If you are more educated than the pastor's wife, please don't get it twisted that you will be a greater pastor's wife than she.

- If your weight and build is that of a "brick house" and the pastor's wife's weight and build is that of a "frame house" or a "warehouse," this does not mean that the "holy" pastor is interested in you. Please sit down!

- Do not invite the pastor over to your home for prayer or a meal without his wife. He can pray for you on the phone. If the pastor is single, let him seek you. He that findeth a wife findeth a good thing is what the Word says. Not she who findeth a husband findeth a good thing. Men notice pretty women and they also notice tumultuous trouble. Many women flock to a single pastor's church, believing the Lord directed them there for marriage. Actually, they can't distinguish the voice of the Lord's from their own voice from the voice of Satan's, but yet they say the Lord led them. As soon as the pastor marries someone outside of the church, they're mad at God because He promised her this man. They're mad at the pastor and mad at the new wife. They will either leave the church or make the pastor's wife miserable and try to prove to the pastor that he missed out by not marrying her. For the lady who truly believed she was the wife to be, but wasn't and is hurting and not mad at anyone, she'll be healed. Remember, if you become a part of the destruction of a marriage, especially a pastor's, you are in trouble with God. Should the pastor's ministry fold, members will be affected greatly. They will be spiritually lost and scattered, along with the pastor's family, which is disappointing to the Lord. I would advise you to store up some forgiveness prayers for yourself so when reaping comes, you'll have easy access to them. You will be too weak at that time to pray fresh prayers. Surely reaping will come; But he that doeth wrong shall receive for the wrong which he hath done: and there is no respect of persons, Colossians 3:25. One lady, who used to date Claxton before my time, was the director of the new member's class and shared with the new members that she dated the pastor. She didn't date the pastor because he was not pastoring at that time. She confused the members and deterred them from church. They didn't join church to hear foolishness. When she first addressed this fabulous idea to Claxton to oversee the new members and he shared it with me, discernment kicked in. I told Claxton her idea was great, but her motive wasn't. I told him she wanted to be the first person to interact with the new members so friendship and trust was developed. Once they met me, they could compare the two of us, yet having a greater appreciation for her, based on the lies she presented about me. Claxton couldn't hear me and didn't believe me until he began getting bad reports, which then opened his eyes. She was telling the members she and I were the best of friends and that I took her man from her. I had never met this woman. Everybody can't oversee baby saints or new members. This is when I wrote the new members' course and orchestrated a team to teach them. It's entitled Walking in Righteousness. She worships at my church now.

- Ushers! When a pastor's wife attends your evening program, please don't assume she wants to be escorted to the front of the church to sit in the designated area; ask her first. Has it dawned on you that she may have on ruined stockings which we call "runny" stockings? Had she stopped to buy some more, she had no place to change into them. She may have her young children with her and they may be acting up. She may have just come to hear the Word for strength for the upcoming week. Who said she's fed by her husband's messages? Who said she hears or listens to her husband as he preaches? Who said she wants to fellowship with the other Pastor's wives? We don't know, do we? I used to attend many services, hoping the MC would not call me up or out. I was there for strength through the Word, not to be seen.

- When planning programs, revivals, dinners or luncheons, remember the sole purpose of any function is to win souls to Christ. Please do not focus on your hair, your nails, your lashes, or your outfit; it's about the souls. You want it done in excellence because the Lord is excellent. Therefore, whatever it takes to make it nice, it is to be done as unto the Lord only. Your choir or lead singer is not in competition with the guest choirs and lead singers. If we are all singing for the Lord, we are all great. We are all winners because we are all winning souls. He that winneth souls is wise, Proverbs 11:30.

- *Humble yourselves in the sight of the Lord. It's God first, then others, then you.* But seek ye first the kingdom of God, and his righteousness; and all these things shall be added unto you, *Matthew 6:33.* Let nothing be done through strife or vainglory; but in lowliness of mind let each esteem other better than themselves, *Philippians 2:3.* My dad instilled in us to keep a low profile and to stay low key and if we took heed, we'd get further along in life than others. When I was older, the revelation came to me that all he was saying to us was to walk in the spirit of humility. We erroneously believe that if a person is quiet, he's humble and if he's extremely outgoing, he's haughty. You have to get my book, *Humbling Thyself!* A person can be quiet while planning great evil.

- If you grew up with the pastor, please don't expect him

to give you special treatment. Once he becomes your spiritual leader, he's just that. You know how quick we are to say how somebody has the "big head" because of a career change or status change. Yes, your brother has changed. He has souls to watch over. He can't socialize like he once did. Wouldn't you want your pastor at home studying, praying, and meditating rather than him attending every sporting event or engrossed in the comedy shows on television or eating at every restaurant in the city? Wouldn't you want to hear that the pastor couldn't attend your function on Saturday night because he was preparing for Sunday? Picture this: You attended church service on Sunday, excited and patiently waiting to hear the message, you're in need of direction, encouragement and healing; the scripture is read and the pastor's message title is so powerful whereas you know your deliverance is coming today through the Word. Some folk are shouting from hearing the title. The pastor gets into the sermon and what he says has no relation to the title, but he's sharing with the church all of the programs he watched on television all week, all the restaurants he ate at and what he ate, and who he saw there, cracking jokes, telling stories, including people from the audience to co-sign his stories and you go home heavier than you were when you left. This should really encourage you to pray for your pastor. Pray that he does not heavily engage in recreation all week whereas he temporarily forgets he's a shepherd and suddenly remembering Sunday morning only to slap something together quickly; a microwave message.

• Everywhere you go, every opportunity you get, invite
someone to the Lord, not necessarily to your church,
but to the Lord. They could already be in attendance
at a church and not know the awesomeness of Jesus.
What's awesome about Jesus? He was beaten for every
sin that we have ever committed; every lie we've
ever uttered, every item we've ever stolen and anyone
we've ever tricked. Jesus took stripes on His back just
for us so we don't have to again live sinful lives. Every
sickness and disease, Jesus took blows so we could be
healed. Then He died on the cross with our sins on His
back so we will never have to die in sin. Then Jesus
was buried and rose again with all power in His hands
after three days. The same power that raised Him from
the dead is the same power that He infused (filled) us
with on the day of Pentecost known as Holy Ghost
power. With this power, we can do greater works than
He. If you don't have it, know that you can be infused
today. Though some say they were filled with the
Holy Ghost once they became believers, Paul asked
some disciples in Acts, Chapter 19 had they received
the Holy Ghost since they believed and they said they
hadn't heard of it. Then Paul asked them how were
they baptized in which they answered, "Unto John's
baptism." Paul clearly let them know that John's
baptism was of repentance and that they are to believe
on the one that comes after him which is Jesus, verse
4. The Bible says when the disciples heard this, they

were baptized in the name of the Lord Jesus. When Paul laid his hands upon them, the Holy Ghost came on them and they spoke with tongues and prophesied. This power is needed to cast out devils, tread over serpents, prophesy, recover the sick and heal all manner of sickness and disease; command, decree and declare; cause the lame to leap and the dumb to sing, open blinded eyes, restore hearing, pray, preach, teach, sing and much more. Isn't that awesome? Having not the Holy Ghost is like sitting in a dark room, reading the Bible. Though our eyes can get adjusted to the darkness, we can only understand the Bible logically and not spiritually. We can't understand it spiritually because we don't have His spirit inside of us. His spirit is just resting upon us, giving us a form of godliness. We can only comprehend spiritual things, spiritually. Because He is a spirit and His spirit is dwelling within us, He'll speak through us to direct us, bring things to our remembrance, comfort us, and teach us. The Holy Ghost is our light in darkness. We are then equipped to understand the Word, the parables and the profound. Ask the Lord to fill you with His Holy Ghost power. Be sure to tell the Lord how sorry you are for your wrongdoing and ask Him to forgive you of every sin you have ever committed. He is waiting to forgive you regardless to how awful you believe your sins are. It does not matter if you've had an abortion, lied, stolen, deceived, envied, fornicated, committed adultery or just full of pride. It doesn't matter if you are currently engaged in these sins. Stop reading right now and speak with Jesus, you can come back to the book. This is repentance; sincerely sorry with a made up mind to live holy. This is the beginning of a new life for you. Peter told us to repent, be baptized in the name of Jesus for the remission of our sins (washing away of our sins) and he promised that we shall receive the gift of the Holy Ghost, Acts 2:38. Believe that this power is real and you will be filled. Say to the Lord, "Show me how real You are. Fill me with Your power, Your Holy Ghost and after I'm filled, I promise I'll tell everyone this power is really real." The evidence of having it is hearing yourself speak another language you did not learn. Shouting is not the evidence. You cannot catch the Holy Ghost power, but you can be infused (filled) with it. That's awesome! Study the book of Acts.

• Live in Holiness - Here's an excerpt on living in holiness from my book entitled Walking in Righteousness:

Living in Holiness means to love God, delighting in godliness. One who lives in holiness is one who worketh righteousness. One who worketh righteousness endeavors to do that which is right or that which is good. The words spoken by an upright man are words of truth; he speaks words of truth in his heart prior to speaking words of truth with his tongue. He closes his ears to slander and backbiting. His focus is to move forward and higher in God by allowing God to be his guide. Nothing or no one can deter him from God or godliness. He shall never give up or go backward. He is forever pressing forward. For he believes that if he should give up, he will never know the journey's end; he will never know what the outcome would have been had he continued to trust and wait on God. A man living in holiness is enthusiastic about hearing the Word of God, studying the Word of God, and living the Word of God. He is always delighted when learning of God; the more he learns, the more he desires to know. When delighted in God, one is never bored. Shame overshadows him when he thinks about living the life he once lived. His conversation is of God. His behavior is of God. Places he found pleasure in are no longer exciting. The conversations with old acquaintances are irritating to his ears and spirit. An upright and holy man is speaking to himself in psalms, hymns, and spiritual songs, making melody in his heart unto the Lord; he awakes each morning with praises unto God on his lips; he daily gives thanks unto the Lord at the remembrance of God's holiness; he magnifies God in prosperity; he glorifies God in poverty; he prays without ceasing, he prays for others; he assembles himself with saints in the sanctuary; he witnesses to others of the wondrous works of God; he testifies of God's grace and mercy; he speaks with love; he responds softly and with compassion, stirring away wrath; he is meek and humble.

Chapter 10

Prayers

Pray for revelation from God for our husbands, pastors and marriages:

Lord, I pray that my husband continues to place You first in every area of his life; I pray that he receives revelation on how to meditate, when to meditate, and where to meditate; I pray that he receives revelation while listening to Your Word for we know faith cometh by hearing, hearing by the Word of Thee; receives revelation while studying Your Word; receives revelation on how to become more dedicated to the ministry and marriage; receives revelation on how to become more loyal to me and to others; receives revelation on how to communicate better with me and others; receives revelation on how to become more understanding, sensitive and loving in disagreements and on how to answer matters; receives revelation on how to become more respectful to me and with others; receives revelation on how to become a greater minister at home first, then with the church; receives revelation on how to develop relationships with our children with loving kindness; receives revelation on how to share with me, remembering we are one; receives revelation on what, how and when to pray with me; receives revelation on how to open up and share deep secrets with me; receives revelation on how to become more considerate of the cares and concerns of mine; receives revelation on how to take the ministry higher; receives revelation on how to win more souls unto You; receives revelation on how to allow the church services to be led by You, Lord and not by a clock, a program, agenda, or a bulletin; receives revelation on how to confront wrongdoers, scorners, gossipers, liars, slanderers, troublemakers, talebearers and the like with love and with Your Word without fear, including me, our parents, friends, siblings, in-laws, other family members and our children; receives revelation on how to admit his faults to me and to himself, immediately repenting so healing takes place; receives revelation on how to endure hardness as a good soldier, together, as one; receives revelation on how to become a better listener to me so we can better resolve issues together; receives revelation on living according to Your Word, loving me as You, Jesus, loves the church; receives revelation on loving me as he loves himself in Jesus' name.

Lord, I pray that I continue to place You first in every area of my life; receive revelation on submitting to my husband and reverencing him; receive revelation on teaching young wives how to love their own husband, how to be keepers of their homes and how to comfort their own husband in Jesus' name.

Lord, I pray that You give pastors revelation on how to consult You concerning church issues; what fast to partake in, what prayer to pray, what scripture to read, what sermon to preach, what songs to sing and what passage of scripture to study; give pastors revelation on who to delegate what to; give pastors revelation on what and how to feed and lead the sheep; give pastors revelation on how to stand on your promises and what promises to stand on in their current situation; give pastors revelation on how to encourage his sheep; give pastors revelation on how to forgive and not just preach on it; give pastors revelation on how to bear one another's burdens; give pastors revelation on training Your sheep on **how not** to walk in the counsel of the ungodly; **how not** to stand in the way of sinners and **how not** to sit in the seat of the scornful; give pastors revelation on training Your sheep on how to delight themselves in the law of the Lord; give pastors revelation on training Your sheep on how to meditate day and night; give pastors revelation on the spirit of Jezebel so it can be recognized and cast out; give pastors revelation on how to recognize the spiritual gifts within the church and how to utilize them; give pastors revelation on allowing their wives to utilize their spiritual gifts without envy; give pastors revelation on how to recognize unclean spirits, immediately casting them out; give pastors revelation on how to allow lay members to go forth in their gifts without intimidation; give pastors revelation on how to allow the sheep to utilize their skills or education without intimidation; give pastors revelation on how to form fasting committees within their churches; give pastors, Pastor's wives, lay members, husbands and wives revelation on walking in the spirit of humility and not pride, haughtiness nor loftiness.

Lord, all of these requests are made in the name of Jesus! Healing, deliverance, salvation, baptism, purification, remission of sin, repentance, conviction and justification all rest in Your name. He who walketh upon the wings of the wind, He who causes water to fall from Heaven as morsels and at Thy rebuke, at Thy Word the morsels melt. That's power! I decree and declare great revelation from Jesus Himself!

Let's pray for all Pastors and Pastor's wives:

Pray that all pastor's wives are respected by the parishioners.

Pray that all Pastor's wives, who are in misery, receive comfort from the Lord.

Pray that the Lord fulfill all Pastor's wives who suffer with loneliness.

Pray that the Lord bestow wisdom upon all Pastor's wives.

Pray that all Pastor's wives prayer lives are increased.

Pray that all Pastor's wives find delight in assisting their husbands in ministry.

Pray that all Pastor's wives exemplify Jesus at all times.

Pray that all Pastor's wives become soul winners.

Pray that all Pastor's wives make more time to study the Word.

Pray that all Pastor's wives are submissive to their husbands.

Pray that all Pastor's wives walk in the spirit of humility.

Pray that all Pastor's wives who walk in pride are humbled.

Pray that all Pastor's wives realize that they are not greater than the women in their church; they are their leader; their example.

Pray that each pastor honors his wife in the presence of her enemies.

Pray that each pastor makes it known to the church that he and his wife are one and are on one accord.

Pray that each pastor balances his time between God, his family and the church.

Pray that each pastor includes his wife in meetings that are comprised of women so that Satan's plans are interrupted.

Pray that each pastor does not become too busy with ministry whereas he's blinded by Satan's tactics.

Pray that each pastor listens to the sayings of his wife; even if he just ponders them.

Pray that each pastor depends upon Jesus only and not man.

Pray that each pastor receives direction from Jesus only and not from all of the prophets within his church, the seasoned saints, the founder's family, the in-laws, the childhood friends or the secretary.

Pray that each pastor is moved by the Spirit of the Lord and not by "a" spirit.

Pray that all Pastor's wives keep personal marital matters outside of the church, if possible.

Pray that God teaches the pastor and his wife how to minister to each other.

Pray that God opens each pastor's heart to receive his wife's revelations, talents, skills and ideas.

More Ways to Pray

Bind and Loose – Whatever is out of order, with authority, lock it up on earth, with words; speak it with your mouth in prayer, in the name of Jesus; that's binding. The Lord said if we bind it here; if we lock it up here, He'll bind it or lock it up in Heaven. Then, whatever our desire is, we must command with authority, that it is released here on earth, in the name of Jesus; that's loosening. The Lord said if we loose it here, He'll loose it in Heaven. That's power! Verily I say unto you, Whatsoever ye shall bind on earth shall be bound in heaven: and whatsoever ye shall loose on earth shall be loosed in heaven, **Matthew 18:18**.

Cast Out – *Speaking to demons with authority, to come out of people.* When the even was come, they brought unto him many that were possessed with devils: and he cast out the spirits with his word, and healed all that were sick, *Matthew 8:16*.

Command – *Speak to unclean spirits and situations with authority:* I command you satan, in the name of Jesus, to come out of her. And this did she many days. But Paul, being grieved, turned and said to the spirit, I **command** thee in the name of Jesus Christ to come out of her. And he came out the same hour, *Acts 16:18*.

Decree – A decision made by one who has authority; a demand; a law; a fact: "Two million copies of my book will be sold; I decree it in the name of Jesus." Thou shalt also **decree** a thing, and it shall be established unto thee: and the light shall shine upon thy ways, **Job 22:28**.

Declare – To speak; to make clear; to set forth; to publish: "I **declare** that two million copies of my book will be sold within one year, in the name of Jesus." I will declare the decree, **Psalm 2:7**.

Life and **Death** are in the power of the tongue, *Proverbs 18:21*.

Speak life to your situations!

Speak death over sin!

Chapter 11

After We Pray

After we pray, which is talking to the Lord, we need to listen to Him. We desire answers to our needs, revelation, direction and instructions from Him directly, we have to find time or make time to listen. Though we receive answers from the Lord through our pastor, spiritual counselors, ministers, books, the Bible, friends, children, songs or television, ain't nothing like receiving a Word directly from Jesus Himself. It's something special about the Lord singling us out just to speak into our spirit. This is how I learned to hear from the Lord. As a child I heard from Him often and followed His direction. I just didn't know who was speaking. I was quiet, always alone, and had no distractions; therefore, I could hear the Lord loudly and clearly. When I grew up, I heard Him, but nothing like I used to. When I became distracted by the cares of the world, friends, clubs, dating, smoking and drinking, fitting in, fashion, cars and the like, that separated me from hearing the voice of the Lord on a regular basis. Please don't misunderstand me. The Lord still spoke to me to warn and inform me, but not daily. It took years for me to desire again what I once had. The Lord gave me revelation knowledge on how to hear Him again daily and I'm sharing it with you.

Psalm 29:3 - The voice of the Lord is upon the waters: the

God of glory thundereth: the Lord is upon many waters.
The voice of the Lord is powerful. When I read this, the
Lord taught me the power of His voice; what His voice
could do; cause trees to stretch out on the ground; cause
flames of fire to divide. If you strike a match or flick your
lighter, the Lord's voice alone can divide the flames. His
voice can shake the earth. His voice directs wild animals
to their meals. His voice causes hail and snow to melt.
His voice causes the earth to be watered for vegetation
and water for the animals to drink and fresh tender grass
for the sheep to eat. His voice is powerful and it is upon
the waters. Therefore, knowing this, sit by the waters
with your notebook and listen for a Word from the Lord.
Get a fountain; allocate some time everyday to hear His
voice. I don't have a fountain yet, so my fountain is the
kitchen sink. I turn on the faucet and let the water run
while I pray, while I read the Bible or while I'm listening
to the Bible. I sit in my living room and commune with
my own heart while the water is running. I turn on the
water in the bathroom when I enter. Out of habit, I turn the
water on in the bathroom while I'm looking for something
in the cabinet or applying make-up. Haven't you heard
of people saying that revelation or songs come to them
while showering? That's the water; that's the voice of the
Lord upon the waters. Haven't you heard people say the
fountains at spas are serene? That's the voice of the Lord.
Isn't the Lord of peace? When you plan to meet the Lord
daily, at the same time, at the same place, He will meet you
there. He wants you to recognize His voice. He does not
want you indecisive as to who is speaking to you. If you

practice this technique, His voice will become distinct just as your spouse's voice, your child's voice or your friend's voice. You are able to recognize their voices only because you have spent time with them. Sometimes I change my voice when my kids call me. They say, "Mama, please, I know your voice." This is how we ought to be when Jesus speaks. When He directs us, no matter the person's voice He uses, we ought to say, "Lord, I know your voice." I encourage you to turn your water on. Are you in a position to turn it on now? Put the book down and finish reading it with the water on. The Lord is not going to speak while we're speaking; that's not communication. He wants us to hear Him. This is how He does me. He speaks between the words I pray or between the words I speak or sing. He speaks during those still moments. When I'm quiet, He speaks. When people say, "Can I ask you something?" I respond and say, "Yes." Then I immediately say to Jesus, but to myself, "Speak through me Lord." As the question is being asked, the Lord is speaking to me, bestowing upon me a wise response even if it's to get back with them later. I said the Lord speaks to me when I'm quiet, not when the speaker is quiet. Remember, the Lord is not going to over talk us and He is not going to fight to get a word in. If we exchange our Masters degree in Talking for a Business School Certificate in Listening, we'd be dangerous.

Chapter 12

Ten-Day Daniel Fast, Daniel 1:8-21

Ten days of vegetables and water!

Benefits:

1. Makes you look better, verse 15.

2. Receive knowledge in all learning from God, verse 17.

3. Receive skill in all learning from God, verse 17.

4. Receive wisdom, verse 17.

5. Understanding in all dreams and visions, verse 17.

6. When conversing, your responses will be different from everyone else's; you stand out above the average, verse 19.

7. Ten times better than magicians, meaning that you will be ten times sharper in Jesus than the magicians are with magic, verse 20.

8. Ten times better than the astrologers, meaning that you will be ten times sharper in Jesus than the

astrologers are with astrology, verse 20.

In addition to what we know to be vegetables, below are foods I eat during this fast:

1. Nuts

2. Hot Cereal (cream of wheat/oatmeal, etc.)

3. Beans (any kind)

4. Rice (cooked any way)

5. Potatoes (cooked in any form)

*Eat as much as you desire to eat and as often as you choose.

*Cook your food as you usually do; it doesn't have to be raw.

*Season your food to taste.

*Prepare your meals in advance.

Fasting is a sacrifice. You're giving up something for God; He's giving up something for you. In the midst of it, Satan distracts and discourages you. Since your spirit is open to receive from the Lord, you become sensitive. If you cry while on this fast, just thank the Lord. This means the fast is effective and affective!

This is an excellent fast to partake in on a regular basis. When fighting the demonic, we have to always be on guard; giving up something for the Lord and waiting for our next move from Him. For years, this was the fast I engaged in because of the many blessings. The first through the tenth of each month was allotted just for this sacrifice unto the Lord. Then there were times when I completed this fast, built my strength up by eating regular meals for a few days, then began the fast again; back to back. You have to be hungry and thirsty for breakthroughs to operate in this realm. We cannot afford to wait on the church fast, even if it's monthly; we have to fast between those fasts. We cannot afford to wait until January to consecrate ourselves when Satan is not waiting until January to attack us. Satan is not playing with us. While we're sitting at the buffet, eating chicken after church, Satan and his partners are planning their attacks against us for the week. We're so busy celebrating the wonderful message the pastor brought that day and how the first soprano songstress tore up the church with the four thousand runs in the song, Satan is already ahead of us while we're focusing on today. We have to strategically fast and pray just as Satan strategically plans his destructive acts against us. We say at church how the devil is defeated and how he can't win because the battle is already won and the devil is a liar and so forth and so on, but we suffer with worry, stress, unfaithfulness to God, deceit, hatred, envy, jealousy, poor prayer lives, financial insolvency, pride, adultery, fornication, lust, covetousness along with everything else contrary to the Word. When we're deceitful, hasn't Satan won? When we're operating in the spirit of jealousy, hasn't Satan won? We cannot double talk nor can we live double lives; we have planning to do!

You will literally hear people say how your countenance is different or how pretty you are while on this fast. Some will say you're glowing and ask questions as to whether or not you're with child or what you're doing because you look different. When you speak, your responses will be different from others. When you write, your words or what you're conveying will stand taller than the norm. Your songs you write will be as the songs of angels. Your learning skills will be as if you are the trainer and not the trainee. Your understanding will be as if the Lord gave only you the revelation. Dreamers, you will have revelation in "all" dreams and visions. You won't need a dream interpretation book. You won't need to call your spiritual advisor; the Lord will speak directly to you. People will want you on their team, in their group, in their pulpit, in their play, in their movie, on their CD, in their presence. People will want you to speak a word over their lives, pray for them, sing or just touch them with your finger. Ain't that powerful? Plan your fast today, not tomorrow! It's urgent!

Chapter 13

Satan is Real, But He's Not

Satan is real in existence, Satan is real in power, Satan is real in wickedness, Satan is a real emulator and Satan is a real simulator, but he is not a real imitator.

Satan's Existence:

Leaders, knowing that Satan goes to and fro in the earth, walking up and down in it, we must increase our prayer lives. This means when we present ourselves before the Lord, Satan comes too, presenting himself. When we make our requests known unto the Lord, Satan makes his, Job Chapter 1. Satan is real in power, but his power is limited. This is because he has to get permission from the Lord to utilize his power.

In Job, Chapter 1, the Lord gave Satan permission to afflict Job. The Lord told Satan to touch Job's possessions only, but not to touch his body. Satan struck Job's oxen, asses, and the servants in verse 14. He burned the sheep and the servants in verse 16. He took the camels and slew the servants in verse 17. In verse 13, Job's kids were eating and drinking at the eldest child's house. In verse 18, Job's kids died. The Lord gave Satan permission to utilize his power. So Satan has power, but it is limited.

Wives, when we're asking the Lord in prayer to strengthen our husbands or to bestow upon him more wisdom, Satan may be saying unto the Lord, "He only fears you because of the blessings that are bestowed upon him and if you take the blessings away, he's going to curse you in your face." The Lord can give him permission to try our husbands. Tests and trials are coming. We will be afflicted. We can cause affliction to come upon ourselves by being disobedient unto the Lord, not adhering to the Lord's voice, commandments and directions. We can allow others to afflict us by following their lead, listening to them. But then God can cause us to be afflicted. Wives, when we know our husbands are living according to the Word of God and he's afflicted, we must pray that our husbands trust the Lord in spite of, so he doesn't give up or give in. If we know our husbands have been clowning and affliction comes upon him, let our prayers be, "Lord, You said whatsoever a man soweth, that shall he also reapeth. So Lord, as my husband reap, help him to handle it and continue to serve Thee. Give him a contrite spirit and, Lord, please forgive him.

In your spare time, read Chapter 2 of Job and you'll learn that Satan had another request of the Lord, which was to afflict Job's body. Satan believed the only reason Job feared the Lord was because his health was good. So read it through. Again, the Lord gave Satan the permission.

Now that we know Satan exists and that he has limited power, know that Satan is real in deception. He deceived many. Remember, Ananias and Sapphira, a husband and wife team who sold a possession and held back some of the money? Peter said unto Ananias, why has Satan filled thine heart to lie to the Holy Ghost, Acts Chapter 5.

Wives, I know we have to stand by our man, but we must stand in truth. Ananias and his wife both concocted a lie and they both died. Satan will make us think there is some right in our wrongdoing. Let us not be deceived. The truth will make us free.

Satan is a Simulator - When I was in high school, I had taken a driver's education class. In the classrooms were simulators. They were small cars with a front seat, a windshield, signals, steering wheel, accelerator, brakes, and ignition. We'd watch a film of a road and pretend we were driving. We actually turned the steering wheel, accelerated, operated brakes, and used turning signals, but we were not moving; we were still. The computer system recorded and printed the errors each simulator made.

This is how Satan is, a simulator, similar to Jesus. He reminds us of Jesus (he speaks to us, sounding similar to Jesus). He can perform similar to Jesus like working miracles, signs, and wonders, Matthew 7:22. Jesus said, "Many will say to me in that day, Lord, Lord, have we not prophesied in thy name? and in thy name have cast out devils? and in thy name done many wonderful works? And then will I profess unto them, I never knew you: depart from me, ye that work iniquity."

This is how we can sometimes be similar to Jesus: looking like we're praying in the presence of others, similar to Jesus; lifting our hands, looking like we're in worship, preaching and teaching His word and not living it, sometimes not believing it. Wives, as we encourage and counsel women in the church, sometimes it's as if what we're saying is from our heart, similar to Jesus. We don't realize that those who seek us for counsel may have spiritual gifts such as discerning of spirits or the gift of the word of knowledge and they know when we're sincere or not. One thing about being a simulator, we ain't going nowhere; we are not moving. Simulators don't move; they just go through the motions.

Satan is an Emulator - An emulator is one who is equal to or higher than another. Isn't this Satan?

How art thou fallen from heaven, O Lucifer, son of the morning! how art thou cut down to the ground, which didst weaken the nations! For thou hast said in thine heart, I will ascend into heaven, I will exalt my throne above the stars of God: I will sit also upon the mount of the congregation, in the sides of the north. I will ascend above the heights of the clouds; I will be like the most High, *Isaiah 14:12-14.*

This is an emulator. Satan was saying that he's going to exalt himself. He said he will be like the Most High.

He's an emulator, desiring to be equal to or greater than God. Emulation is sin. Galatians 5:19-21 lists emulations as one of the works of the flesh, which is really the spirit of pride. Some pastors are emulators and sometimes Pastor's wives are emulators and sometimes the pastor and his wife emulates as a team. The Bible says we shall not inherit the kingdom of God if we do these things.

"Now the works of the flesh are manifest, which are these; adultery, fornication, uncleanness, lasciviousness, idolatry, witchcraft, hatred, variance, emulations, wrath, strife, seditions, heresies, envyings, murders, drunkenness, revellings, and such like: of the which I tell you before, as I have also told you in time past, that they which do such things shall not inherit the kingdom of God."

We know Satan is real in existence, real in power, though it is limited, and real in deception.

Satan is Real, but He's Not!

Satan is a real **simulator** of Jesus—he does things similar to God.

Satan is a real **emulator** of Jesus—he desires to be equal to or greater than God.

One thing Satan is not and that is an **imitator** of Jesus. If he was an imitator, there would be no Satan. If Satan imitated Jesus, not if he was similar to Him or equal to or greater than Jesus, but actually imitated Him, there would be no enemy, there would be no prince of the power of the air; there would be no power of darkness, there would be no ruler of darkness, there would be no adversary, or murderer, no devil, or prince of this world, or father of lies, or evil spirits, or unclean spirits, or antichrist.

The Lord gave me an analogy using vanilla flavoring to bring clarity to simulation, emulation and imitation; showing how powerful imitation is.

My Analogy – Vanilla Flavoring

Imagine two bottles of vanilla flavoring; one bottle is pure vanilla, the other is imitation vanilla. Both bottles are shaped the same, both bottles hold the same amount of ounces; both bottles have a white label on them; both bottles hold brown substance, both look just alike; same consistency; one is not thicker than the other; they both smell alike; taste alike and do the same work. They can be purchased at the same store, and they sit on the same shelf. Well, what's the difference? The difference is one has pure vanilla written on it, the other has imitation vanilla written on it. We aren't being deceived, we aren't tricked. We know the bottle of imitation vanilla has imitation written on it. The pure vanilla costs more of course and this is because it represents Jesus Christ, the imitation vanilla represents us, the saints, doing what Jesus does, imitating Him.

One thing about Satan is, he does not have written upon

himself "imitation." He makes us think he's pure and wants us to believe it. On some of the vanilla flavoring bottles, the word imitation is written extremely small in parenthesis, but nevertheless, it is written. Nowhere on Satan is imitation written. This is because he is an emulator and a simulator, not an imitator.

Let us not be like Satan, but more and more like Jesus Christ, imitating Him. We are to sound like Jesus, we are to leave an aroma, sweet-smelling savour like Jesus when we enter or exit a room. Let us cast out demons, imitating Jesus, let us walk uprightly, imitating Jesus, let us consecrate ourselves, imitating Jesus, let us pray, let us be kind one to another, let us be full of compassion, let us rest in the midst of our storm, imitating Jesus. Let us walk in the spirit of humility, let us preach and teach, let us live in peace, let us trust in God, let us possess a skill, imitating Jesus, let us work miracles, signs and wonders, and let us be holy daily, not weekly, imitating Jesus.

Pastor's wives, let us imitate Jesus in everything we do. I know you don't like imitation purses, furs, leather coats, jewelry and shoes. But this imitation is good; everyone will desire it. It's something how we like authenticity until it comes to our hair, nails, lashes, make-up and girdles. Just like we make appointments to have hair attached upon our heads and we want it just right so onlookers will think it's the real thing. That's how we are to be when it comes to Jesus. When we are in the presence of others, they ought to feel as if Jesus is upon us. They ought to say it seems as if Jesus is present. Be an imitator of Christ, not a simulator which goes nowhere or an emulator, which is a sin.

Chapter 14

Sweeter Than Honey

The full soul loatheth an honeycomb; but to the hungry soul every bitter thing is sweet, *Proverbs 27:7*.

The full soul is one who attends church services with the expectation of the working of miracles, being in God's presence, hearing God's Word, receiving God's Word, applying God's Word, and sharing God's Word, discussing it, teaching it, preaching it and witnessing it.

The full soul finds great joy in learning more or all he can about God; Jesus said in Matthew 11, "Learn of Me."

The full soul finds delight in the law of the Lord in both day and night. Day, when all is well; money is in the account; children are obedient; children are doing well in school; bills are paid and paid on time; no trouble on the job; marriage is great; in-laws are a blessing and not a curse; no trouble with the car or home repairs to be made. And then in the night, a full soul finds delight in the law of the Lord. Night, when ain't no money left after the bills are paid; ain't no money to pay all of the bills for the month; robbing Peter to pay Paul, Paul has an attitude cause he can't have it all; Paul is blowing up the phone; kids are clowning; marriage is failing; trouble on every hand; from the home to the in-laws to the job to the school.

The full soul encourages himself as David encouraged himself in the Lord. He also encourages others without lying. You know how the saints do, tell the singer she did a great job just to encourage her when in actuality the singing was a mess. The full soul wants the singer to be full too, so he tells her she needs to consecrate herself so she can do more with her voice for the Lord. The full soul loves at all times, without dissimulation, even with his neighbors.

The full soul studies to shew himself approved and not to show others that he can prove. He studies the Word, not to argue with others concerning the scriptures, not to make others think he is knowledgeable of God's written Word, not to make himself feel superior to babes in Christ and not to feel intellectual. He studies to know the ways and the works of God for personal growth and to be more knowledgeable to win souls to Christ with love, kindness, compassion and humility.

The full soul is often found meditating upon the Word of God. He finds quiet time just to hear from the Lord directly, for direction.

The full soul moves when God says move and speaks when God says speak.

The full soul has an ear to hear and a heart to understand God and His Word.

The full soul thinks on things that are true, whatsoever things are honest, whatsoever things are just, whatsoever things are pure, whatsoever things are lovely, whatsoever things are of good report. He thinks on Heavenly things, and finds delight in music that makes him think on Heavenly things.

The full soul recognizes the voice of the Lord so well whereas he can cast out the foolish thoughts Satan places in his mind and follow it with a Word from the Lord.

The full soul does not engage in foolish conversations because he feels that if he takes time to listen to anything, it will be in meditation, awaiting the Lord; and when the full soul speaks, it is pleasant, uplifting, kind, upgrading and not degrading.

The full soul is full at all times, not just on Sundays, prayer nights, and Bible class nights.

The full soul is full of the nine gifts of the Spirit in Galatians 5:22: love, joy, peace, longsuffering, gentleness, goodness, faith, meekness and temperance.

The full soul continuously walks in the spirit of humility, casting out the spirit of haughtiness, pride or loftiness.

The full soul sings to the Glory of God and for the Glory of God.

The full soul is giving, forgiving, caring, and always helpful.

The full soul's light shines brightly as he enters a room.

The full soul prays without ceasing.

The full soul fasts, prays, praises, worships, meditates and consecrates himself.

The full soul gives honor where honor is due.

The full soul does not hold fast to the wicked, but yet overthrows the righteous.

The full soul's words are as a honeycomb, sweet to the soul, health to the bones.

Now that you have a better understanding of "The Full Soul," let me tell you about the honeycomb.

The full soul **loatheth an honeycomb**, but to the hungry soul, every bitter thing is sweet, Proverbs 27:7.

Loatheth An Honeycomb - Loatheth means to dislike greatly; despise; hate; detest, can't stand.

Honeycomb - A honeycomb is made up of a mass of cells, hexagonal shaped or a shape consisting of six sides, made up of beeswax produced by bees. The honeycomb s the internal wall of the bee hive. Honey is stored in the honeycomb. When each cell is filled with honey, the bees cover the cell with wax, which is called capping the cell.

This means that the full soul is not going to hang around honeycombs.

The honeycomb appears to be good because honey is good and sweet. When we hang around the honeycombs, we can be stung by bees.

The full soul deters from the honeycomb.

The full soul is so busy enjoying Jesus; he has no time to think about what's happening in the honeycomb or what's happening with the honeycomb. A lot of things happen in the honeycomb besides the storing of honey. The queen bee lays an egg in each cell of the honeycomb; the larva (young insects) develops in the cells; bees gather nectar and pollen to feed the young which are in the cells. Remember, the full soul's delight is in the law of the Lord.

The full soul is consistently drawing sap from the rivers of water because he is like the tree planted by the rivers of water. That tree is Jesus. We are all to be like Him. We must imitate Him. I wrote a song and the lyrics within the song say, "Jesus is the vine and Jesus is the tree, the sap that flows from Him, is the power in me."

The honeycomb is built by the bees; that's beeswax; the

honey is produced by the bees; and the honeycomb stores the honey.

The full soul stays away from the honeycomb because he is full. Honey is sometimes too sweet, too thick, too rich and filling. The full soul is satisfied; he's content.

The full soul loathe an honeycomb, but to the hungry soul every bitter thing is sweet, Proverbs 27:7.

But to the hungry soul, every bitter thing is sweet.

The hungry soul is one who is not satisfied with anything. His appetite is great, but after eating, he is still hungry. It's sort of like how we are after eating fried rice; as soon as we get home, we're hungry. Nothing seems to hit the spot. He can always eat a little more. Always! He's never full.

The hungry soul hasteth to be rich and hath an evil eye and considereth not that poverty shall come upon him, Proverbs 28:22. The Bible says, In all labour there is profit: but unrighteous labor is temporary great gain and all unrighteousness is sin. Unto the hungry soul, the more money he earns, the more he thinks he needs to earn. He's never satisfied. Remember, he's hungry!

Because of his hunger, he'll eat anything; he hangs around the honeycomb.

The hungry soul will eat honey from the honeycomb;

that's the churches that preach and teach false doctrine; he follows because every bitter thing is sweet.

The hungry soul will eat honey from the honeycomb; that's the false prophets who come to the great revivals; he follows because every bitter thing is sweet.

The hungry soul will eat honey from the honeycomb; that's the sermons teaching against paying tithes; sermons teaching that fasting is not for today; sermons teaching against the infilling of the Holy Ghost with the evidence of speaking in other tongues; sermons teaching that everyone will enter Heaven; sermons teaching that healing is not taking place today, but was only practiced in Biblical days; the hungry soul follows because every bitter thing is sweet. Remember, he hangs around the honeycomb so anything that passes by him; he follows because every bitter thing is sweet.

All of this bitterness seems sweet to the hungry soul!

The hungry soul searches for satisfaction, wasting time, energy, and money when all he has to do is search for He who created the bee and taught the bee to build the honeycomb, taught the bee to make the honey. He is our Creator, He is our Savior, He is our Anointed One, He is all Power, He is all Knowing, He is our Counselor, He is our Keeper, He is our Prayer Hearer, He is our Prayer Answerer, He is our Lord, He is Jesus Christ, Sweeter than Honey.

After the hungry soul gets done traveling, after he gets done spending; after he gets done giving; after he gets done conferencing; after he gets done trusting every wind of doctrine; after his disgust; after his disappointment; after his busyness, he has nothing to show for it but bee stings. He hangs around the honeycomb, but he never gets any of the honey.

Now some hungry souls get a chance to taste the honey after hanging around the honeycomb only to find out that the honey was not good, kind of like the clover honey where the bees extract clover from the clover plant. And after all of that hard work, the hungry soul is still hungry, not only is he hungry, he's tired!

Husbands, wives, men, women, be the full soul. The full soul seeks counsel. The full soul has a mentor. He shares his troubles and won't pretend he's exempt from them. He's transparent and wants his sheep to know where he came from, how he used to be, how God delivered him and he's not ashamed to tell it because he's free and wants his sheep to know the Lord will do the same for them.

Husbands, wives, men, women, be the full soul and always trust in **He** who created the bee. He is sweeter than honey, Jesus Christ!

Chapter 15

Some Are Cursed, Some Are Blessed

T hus saith the LORD; Cursed be the man that trusteth in man, and maketh flesh his arm, and whose heart departeth from the LORD, *Jeremiah 17:5-8*.

Three Curses:

Curse I - Cursed be the man that trusteth in man.

Why are we cursed? Because man changes. If all of our trust is in man and man should pass away, so does our trust. A job change can change a man; a marriage or divorce can change a man; weight gain or weight loss can change a man; prosperity or poverty can change a man; so why rest our trust in man? Man will change a plan at any time and not tell you. Man will call at 7 o'clock when you asked him to call at 5 o'clock. Man will come to meet you at 9 o'clock with a friend when you asked him to meet you at 3 o'clock alone. Man will prophesy to you and lie on you in the same hour. Man will tell you what you don't need to buy and then go out and buy it for himself. Man will compliment you and complain about the compliment he gave you in the same breath. Man will lie on you and to you in the same sentence. Man will give you an award, dig into your history to find dirt, and then snatch the award back and broadcast it. Man will build you up and tear you down the next day. Isn't this what happened to Jesus? Hosanna; Blessed is he that cometh in the name of the Lord: Blessed be the kingdom of our father David, that cometh in the name of the Lord: Hosanna in the highest. Then in all four of the Gospels the same people shout, Crucify Him!

Curse II – Cursed be the man maketh flesh his arm.

Why are we cursed? We are cursed because we are making flesh (which is man) our arm (which is strength). The strength of man can easily be decreased; decreased spiritually and physically. The strength of man can be decreased spiritually by lack of prayer, lack of hearing God's Word, which decreases man's faith; lack of studying God's Word; lack of fasting; lack of meditating; and the lack of worshipping. The strength of man can be decreased physically by the lack of exercising; improper eating, under eating or overeating; illness; lethargy or slothfulness. This is why we can't make flesh our strength. Flesh weakens.

Curse III – Cursed be the man whose heart departeth from the Lord.

When our heart departs from the Lord, we are then walking in the imagination of own heart; making our own decisions; consulting no one; seeking no counsel; I'm grown, I can do what I want to do. As I tell my children, there are rules everywhere you go: at school, at work, in our township, at home and there are also consequences for not abiding by the rules. I have to follow rules too as grown as I am, and if not there are consequences for me to suffer as well. The rules for life are written in the Bible, if we do not follow them, we must suffer consequences. We must draw closer to the Lord daily and never depart from Him. The closer we draw to the Lord, the more we'll trust Him, trusting not our own heart. He that trusteth in his own heart is a fool: but whoso walketh wisely, he shall be delivered, Proverbs 28:26.

If we are going to be cursed, wouldn't you like to know how? For he shall be like a heath in a desert, and shall not see when good cometh; but shall inherit the parched places in the wilderness, in a salt land.

A heath is a bush. Deserts are hot and dry. If our trust is in man, if we're making flesh our strength, and if we depart from the Lord, we shall be like a bush growing in dry land and not as a tree planted by the rivers of water.

And Shall Not See When Good Cometh. Because our trust is in man and all we're hearing is the intellect of the man whom we trust, whether it's our educated children, our parents, our professors, best friend, our older sibling or whomever. If these are the people whom we give ear to for all of our needs, when the Lord sends a wind of wisdom or a wind of prophecy or a wind of the Word of knowledge, we will not believe it, we will not accept it. We would call those words of God hogwash. When blessings are right before us, we'll miss them because our trust is in others. The Lord can speak a Rhema Word directly into our spirits while we're in a room alone in quietness and we won't receive it because it didn't come from the people whom we trust.

Be in a position to see the good come and when it comes, receive it.

But Shall Inhabit (dwell in) or (live in) **The Parched** (dried up, scorched, burnt up) **Places in the Wilderness** (woods, boondocks), **In A Salt Land** (barren or unfruitful) **And Not Inhabited** (unpopulated) (by yourself). This is a hearty consequence to suffer for trusting in man, making him our strength, and departing from the Lord.

The Blessing – Blessed is the man that trusteth in the Lord, and whose hope the Lord is.

The Lord is his trust and his hope. Though trouble comes, when we trust in the Lord, our hope is in Him because our faith is in Him. This hope is not maybe He will, maybe He won't. It's not a wish either. It's a surety; it's a sure thing; it's confidence; having confidence in the Lord.

As for God, his way is perfect; the word of the LORD is tried: he is a buckler to all them that trust in him, II *Samuel 22:31.*

The fear of man bringeth a snare: but whoso putteth his

trust in the LORD shall be safe, *Proverbs 29:25.*

Every word of God is pure: he is a shield unto them that put their trust in him, *Proverbs 30:5.*

Trust ye in the LORD for ever: for in the LORD JEHOVAH is everlasting strength, *Isaiah 26:4.*

The LORD is good, a strong hold in the day of trouble; and he knoweth them that trust in him, *Nahum 1:7.*

Trust the Lord, it doesn't matter what you're faced with. It doesn't matter who has done what, who is doing what, when they did it or whether or not anyone knows about it. Trust ye the Lord today. Trust the Lord, stand on His promises always. Don't ever get tired of doing right.

Remember that man changes, but God changes not. Don't dwell on your situation, lay them on the altar and begin to praise God for your victory and then intercede in prayer for someone else who may be going through.

For he shall be as a tree planted by the waters, and that spreadeth out her roots by the river and shall not see when heat cometh, but her leaf shall be green and shall not be careful in the year of drought, neither shall cease from yielding fruit.

When we are as a tree planted by the waters, we are full of sap, full of life, full of power, full of Jesus; our well will never run dry. When we are planted by the waters, we are soaking up the Word of God every chance we get. Every opportunity we get, we're hearing God's Word; we're meditating, waiting to hear from the Lord. When our roots are spreadeth out by the river, we are growing stronger in Jesus because we become deeper in Him, deeply rooted in Him. The roots that are spread by the river consists of the knowledge, the understanding, the revelation, and the wisdom that God has bestowed upon us whereas we have much to teach, much to testify about and we can minister to many. Roots can be hidden. Though we can't always see the roots, they have great strength. Because roots can be hidden, we don't always know who is full of wisdom. Even a tall tree cannot be looked upon as full of revelation; a large tree does not mean it's full of knowledge. One thing for sure, a tree is known by its fruit.

Speaking of wisdom, because Claxton is so smart, so educated and so knowledgeable of the Word, I was outdone at his behavior on many occasions. Let me hit you with some:

a. Claxton shared with my close friend that he found out that we were not married after 10 years. He had found the marriage documents hidden in our former pastor's desk drawer that hadn't been mailed to the county. He said he wasn't going to tell me because I would have been hurt. She said, "So you're going to let her think she's married, but really you all are shacking?" He said, "Yes." She said, "Are you going to marry her now that you know?" He said, "No, Lord." She was devastated and felt obligated to tell me, though he told her not to. She didn't want me to live in sin. I went to the courts to see about it. I was upset because I suffered for years with someone I wasn't married to. When the clerk said we were married, I almost slapped her for checking. I was just as mad to learn we were really still married as I was to learn we weren't. That was an unnecessary lie.

b. When our daughter was about three or four years old, she knew what to say to get Claxton upset. So one day she met him at the door when he came in from work and told him I had body slammed her. She went and got her baby doll and demonstrated how I slammed her down. She also said I called her names. He believed her and he clowned a while with me. I said, "You believe I slammed my child on the floor?" His answer was yes. Can you believe that? Then he came up with this revelation that we are not supposed to whip kids and we have been misunderstanding what the Bible meant by rod. He said the rod meant "time out" or to remove a toy. After she'd stir him up every day, then she'd go to her room, get under the cover and laugh. He sat down and tried to reason with our daughter about why she probably got hit by me. She was about three years old. Finally, Claxton caught on to the devil using her to cause confusion between us. This was the answer. He didn't want any of the kids to be hit ever again and he threatened me.

c. When my Mom was sick, she lived with us for almost two years. The saints were angry about that. Yes, about my Mom living with me. They said she was distracting Claxton from ministry work. My mom had breast cancer, but she was still cooking, cleaning and everything else. Claxton was crazy about her. When she moved back to her home, she got worse. I was taking her to and from her doctor's appointments, treatment centers, pharmacy and wherever she needed me to go. I was back and forth. When she was admitted in the hospital, I stayed the night, went home in the mornings to get my kids together, came back to the hospital, went back to get dinner ready, then came back to stay the night. I was so tired, but I didn't complain. All of my siblings worked and I didn't, so I was the only one available. My mom was always in a good spirit. She never complained. She encouraged the nurses and all of her visitors. She prophesied to the people while taking oral pain medicine, pain shots and pain patches. One evening, the doctor told me my mom had six months to live; I nearly passed out. I had to leave the hospital after that blow. I sat in my car for a while in awe. I was thinking, "Who could I call?" That shouldn't have taken much thought. I called Claxton. My heart was racing. I could hardly dial his number. He said, "Hello." I said, "Claxton, where are you?" I was going to meet him wherever he was because I was really low. I don't get low often. He said, "In Baltimore." I said, "Balti who?" "Baltimore, getting me some rest." Did you hear me say I was travelling back and forth to the hospital, cooking and so on? He was getting him some rest. He didn't even come to the hospital. He said, "Them doctors don't know what they're talking about; your Mama ain't going nowhere." Are y'all still stuck on Baltimore? He said he'd be back in a few days. Mama died two months later; the doctors knew something. I knew he wasn't a prophet. Then when she passed, it was on a Sunday morning, in her home. He didn't come over. He went to church and preached. Maybe that was how he dealt with his grief. He did preach her funeral, but he blocked the repast committee from buying food for the repast. The mother of the church bought the food with her own money and brought her dishes and silver place settings from home to make it really nice for my family.

d. Claxton hired a maid—an elderly woman. Wasn't that nice? What woman wouldn't want a maid? This freed up my day. Wasn't that thoughtful of him? Well, she only cleaned his side of the room, his office and the bathroom in his office. Wasn't that special? This was not discussed with me. He purchased all new cleaning supplies just for her to use on his stuff. When her brand new vacuum cleaner broke, she called me up out of my bedroom to tell me. I told her she needed to take that up with her supervisor. I told her to tell him to get her a Kirby and she would not have these problems. One week I didn't see her, so when she came the following week something told me ask her why she didn't come the week prior. She said because I didn't pick her up. That's what Pastor told her. I said, "Why would I drive across town to pick you up to clean up for him?" I told her the next time she takes on a job, working for a married couple, she needs to meet with the wife. I told her she is not to come up in another woman's house and start cleaning without the okay from both parties. She never returned. You know what else? He used to have the car detailer come to our house to detail his car only.

e. Early in our marriage, I was cooking breakfast for Claxton. I cooked a whole spread. I made his plate and was cleaning up the kitchen. He started frowning as he was eating. I knew the food couldn't have been awful; after all, it was just breakfast. I said, "What's wrong?" He said, "The food." "The food, what?" "The grits." "The grits, what?" "You cain't cook them, they are not like Mama's." "How does your mama make them?" "With a whole lot of lumps, different sizes of lumps." I'm thinking, "Different sizes?" He said, "You cain't cook." I said, "I just don't know how to make lumpy grits, but I'll cook some more." Here I am purposely trying to cook grits incorrectly. I'm struggling, trying to figure this puzzle out. Who was I going to call and ask how to make lumpy grits? When I handed him the bowl, he said, "Yeah, this looks more like Mama's, like meatballs." He started eating it and got to the good part, the lump. He cracked one of the lumps open and dry grits popped out and went all over the table; I heard them hit the table. He was mad because I messed up his breakfast with my non-cooking self. Here I am nervous because I didn't fix the food right. You know how you want the best for your husband? He said, "Don't fix me no more grits cause you cain't cook." I was holding back and I just had to say it. I said, "My parents owned nursing homes, restaurants, and catered. I know my people can cook. I cooked for the senior citizens in fifth grade. I learned how to cook for large groups in grade school. What you don't know is that your Mama cain't cook. Don't ever tell anyone you like lumpy grits because everybody will know that your cooking instructor needed lessons. And please don't request lumpy grits at the restaurant. And you're right, I cain't cook. I cain't cook lumpy grits and I'll never try again. Sitting at the head of the table, complaining, eating white meatballs."

Claxton made man his strength. Oftentimes, his advice came from people and not God. His trust was in people, not the Lord. When our trust is solely in the Lord, we shall not see when heat cometh. This is because we'll be so wrapped up in Jesus and wrapped up in Heavenly things, when heat comes, when trouble comes, when our child is in trouble, when our loved one passes away, when sickness comes, it won't cause us to lose sleep or to lose our appetite or to lose or gain weight. It won't cause us to lose our mind either. The Bible says we won't see when the heat comes. This is because when our troubles come, they're just there. The troubles hit us right then. When they arrive, we attack them immediately in prayer or in prayer and fasting. The Lord will show us things to come or He will show us trouble to come in dreams whereas we can store up some prayers; however, we still won't see the heat coming, though the Lord told us its coming; when it comes, it'll just be present. He can also speak a Word of knowledge to our spirits as to what's going on right now, but even in this case we still didn't see it coming, though God spoke to us, saying that this issue is happening now. One thing about God's power is, when our heat does come, it'll be like a knife gliding across our skin, but as it is cutting, God is healing us at the same time. That's power!

Pastor's wives, ministers' wives, hurting wives, wives, ministers, our leaves shall be green if we are as a tree planted by the waters. Not brown, not withered, not wilted, not dry, not weak, not brittle, but green, flourishing, alive!

We do not have to be concerned with storing up food, storing up water, storing up gasoline, storing up household commodities or anything else because we will always have. All of our needs will be met because our trust is in the Lord.

We will always produce fruit, nothing will stop us, nothing will deter us, and nothing can stop us. Our trust is in God, He is our hope, our leaves are green, and we're as a tree, not a bush. Trees produce fruit and seeds are in the fruit, which means the tree will replenish. Bushes don't carry fruit, therefore, there are no seeds and no seeds mean no producing nor reproducing. Let our roots spread out by the rivers being filled with the knowledge of God, being filled with the wisdom of God, being filled with the understanding of God, being filled with revelation of God so when trouble comes, we'll be full of strength that only comes from God, to handle any matter.

If you are cursed, know that you can be blessed today. God is no respecter of persons. This means God will bless all of us!

You don't have to be rich to be blessed. You don't have to be educated to be blessed. You don't have to be a pastor's wife to be blessed. You don't have to be a pastor to be blessed. All you have to do to be blessed is trust in the Lord and do His will; make Him your strength, not man.

When we trust in the Lord, we shall be protected, we shall be safe, we shall be fed, and we shall not be removed. The Lord will be our shield, He shall be our help.

Trust in the LORD with all thine heart; and lean not unto thine own understanding, *Proverbs 3:5.*

Trust in the Lord, Pastor's wives. Trust in the Lord, Pastors. Trust in the Lord, Elders. Trust in the Lord, hurting wives. Trust in the Lord, hurting leaders.

When we trust in the Lord, we shall abide forever!

Some Are Blessed, Some Are Cursed, Be Blessed!

Chapter 16

Righteously Speaking

The lips of the righteous feed many; but fools die for want of wisdom, *Proverbs 10:21.*

As leaders, we are spokesmen and spokeswomen for the Lord. Therefore, we must be careful of the words that proceed out of our mouths. Wisdom, which only comes from God, must proceed from our mouths.

Encouragement, at all times, must proceed from our mouths. Leaders shouldn't say what they want to say because they have the authority to do so. It is imperative for us to be led by God to speak. Leaders can't say what they want to say because the microphone is in their hand; the microphone is not to be used as a power tool.

Let's define the righteous - The righteous are the good, just, honest, and truthful people.

In Psalm 15, David asked the Lord a question; Lord, who shall abide in thy tabernacle; who shall dwell in thy holy hill? The Lord answered saying, he that walketh uprightly and worketh righteousness.

He that walketh upightly is one who constantly and consistently endeavors to do that which is right. His labor is not to impress God or others, but he labors because of the desire he has to follow God. His reason for walking uprightly is because he finds delight in serving God.

He that worketh righteousness is one who is not silent in the presence of unrighteousness (the Bible says the righteous are bold as a lion). He has backbone and stands up for righteousness. He is caring, thoughtful, gentle, and just simply nice. He will not wrong men; trickery is not in his heart. Righteousness does not mean one is perfect. Jesus is righteous, Jesus is perfect, we're following Him, and we're imitating Him. We must daily purify ourselves, cleansing our minds of ugly thoughts, daily repenting. A perfect man would not have to do this.

Be ye therefore perfect, even as your Father which is in heaven is perfect, *Matthew 5:48*.

Be ye therefore perfect means we must be imitators of the perfect One, Jesus Christ. We must act like Him and in His likeness, daily.

God made the sun to rise on the good and the evil and He sent rain to fall upon the just and the unjust. This means when He blesses, He blesses the righteous people and the unrighteous people. He blesses the saved people and the unsaved people.

Example - Let's take two farmers, living in the same city, both growing corn, grapes and coffee; one farmer is living holy and faithful to God in every way whereas the other farmer is an atheist. Both farmers need rain; the saved farmer and the unsaved farmer. Because of the goodness of God, He causes rain to pour onto both fields. If we had the power or authority to pour down rain, some of us would make some fields become deserts. This is not how God operates, like some of us would. God wants us to be imitators of Him. He knows we're going to love our family and friends; but the greatness is in His commandment, love your enemies. God knows we will pray for those who treat us well; but the greatness is in His commandment, pray for those who despitefully use you and persecute you. God knows we're going to bless the person who blesses us; but the greatness is in His commandment, bless them that curse you. God knows we're going to do good to our loved ones, but the greatness is in His commandment, do good to them that hate you.

This is walking in the Spirit of perfection, walking in righteousness.

Once we enter Heaven, we can then say we are perfect, until then, we are maturing.

Now that we have a greater knowledge of what a righteous man or a righteous woman is, let me make my point. The lips of the righteous feed many, but fools die for want of wisdom.

There are three keys in Righteously Speaking:

Key I - Speak for Jesus:

And he said unto them, Go ye into all the world, and preach the gospel to every creature, *Mark 16:15.*

God wants us to preach His Word to everyone regardless to their age, race, education level, title or last name.

Speaking for Jesus means to meditate so we can hear His voice and speak the words He gives us with nothing added and nothing taken away.

Jesus said, What I tell you in darkness, that speak ye in light: and what ye hear in the ear, that preach ye upon the housetops, *Matthew 10:27.*

We are not to keep to ourselves that which Jesus speaks to us. Our speech is to be always with grace, seasoned with salt; that we may know how we ought to answer every man. This means when we're speaking for Jesus, our words are to always be tasteful. The words we speak are to be to the listener, kind, comforting, compassionate, pleasant, peaceful, and with wisdom whereas their response is, I've never heard it said like that before or I'll never forget that or I'm in awe at what was said. Speaking for Jesus is speaking things that you know and testifying of the things you have seen. Speaking for Jesus is speaking the truth in our hearts. We are to be honest in our speech at all times. If someone asks our opinion, speak the truth. The world teaches that when you have to reprimand a subordinate in private, use a technique that will not hurt. Say something good that was done, then top it with the purpose of the meeting, and then cover it with something that was appreciated, even if you have to concoct something or create something in your mind to tell them; that's deception. If we are speaking for Jesus, be direct. Before the meeting, pray, asking Jesus to assist you. Remember, we must speak the truth in our heart. The same with compliments: Speak the truth and the same goes with encouraging. Please don't tell a singer that you were blessed by a song sang, and you weren't; that's not encouragement, that's lying. If you must say something or if you're obligated to say something, just say, "God bless you!" as you're hugging them. If you really want to encourage them, speak the truth, whatever it is. It will be appreciated later. Speaking for Jesus requires speaking softly to avoid wrath, speak with surety when witnessing, speak to unclean spirits, sickness, diseases, troubles and pain with authority; holy boldness!

Key II – Speak Beneath Jesus: Spirit of Humility

Speak, knowing that all of your direction, guidance and help comes from the Lord and not self. Speak knowing that when we boast and brag about what we have, what we're getting, where we're going, where we've been, what we've done, what we're doing, etc., God hears us and He's in the process of snatching it back. God wants us to give Him honor for all that we have and all that we do. Speak knowing that God is the Most High and we are the most low, regardless to our backgrounds, education, honors, titles, experiences, finances, where we reside or the make and model of our cars.

When we exalt ourselves, great strength is required. When we do this, we don't have as much strength to come down. Since God's strength is great, He'll handle it for us, He'll bring us down; He'll humble us with no problem as He did with King Nebuchadnezzar in Daniel Chapter 4. God is no respecter of persons. If we walk in the spirit of humility, we'll automatically speak beneath Jesus (in humility). We cannot speak to people as if we're greater than them or as if they are beneath us. The message we're trying to convey to them will not be received. We have to assure our listeners that we are all riding on the same boat (share testimonies), singing the same song (share struggles or issues you're faced with at home). This way, their minds are opened to receive the Word from us. We are as a blade of grass, a withered flower and filthy rags according to God and this is how we are to present ourselves when standing before God's people. Speak beneath Jesus.

Key III – Speak to Jesus

Speak to Jesus in prayer - Pray in the Spirit, and then ask God to interpret what was said. Pray for others (interceding). Pray without ceasing. Pray for your enemies. Pray the scriptures. Pray in the evening, at noon and in the morning. Pray effectual (powerful or having the force behind your intended results). Pray fervently (sincere, earnest, holy zeal, burning with excitement). Pray for the leaders to have a peaceable life. Pray for your friends as Job did. Pray three times per day as David did. Pray for your persecutors. Pray for your haters. Pray always. Speak for Jesus, Speak beneath Jesus and Speak to Jesus.

With these three keys, you will have the lips of the righteous and you shall feed many not just at church but at the mall, the grocery store, the gym, the park, the laundry mat, at school, the bank and at work.

The Lord wilt bless the righteous; with favour. The mouth of the righteous speaketh wisdom. The LORD loveth the righteous.

The lips of the righteous feed many but fools die for want of wisdom. Fools despise wisdom and instruction. The mouth of fools feedeth on foolishness.

The fool hath said in his heart, There is no God. They are corrupt, they have done abominable works, there is none that doeth good, *Psalm 14:1.*

A fool can become righteous today; he does not have to stay in this state; the state of foolishness. Repent, tell God you're sorry for everything you've done wrong, including what you have forgotten, be baptized in the name of Jesus, receive the gift of the Holy Ghost, learn how to live holy on a daily basis from a pastor.

Chapter 17

Afflicted to Pray

Before I was afflicted I went astray: but now have I kept Thy Word, *Psalm 119:67.*

Is any among you afflicted? Let him pray, *James 5:3.*

Affliction - Distress; suffering; persistent pain; a state of misery; mental or bodily pain as sickness, loss or calamity; oppression; tribulation; anguish; burden.

Affliction is the beginning of longsuffering. Longsuffering is a bitter piece of fruit that becomes sweet.

The Bible doesn't tell us what the psalmist did when he went astray. I wonder what he was doing. What do we do when we go astray? He could have been mistreating his wife. He could have abandoned his family. He could have stopped praying or trusting the Lord. What we do know is that he was afflicted. The Bible doesn't tell us what his affliction was either. It could have been any manner of sickness or disease; nevertheless, he was afflicted.

The Bible then says but now have I kept Thy Word. The psalmist said, "Now I'm standing on Thy Word. Now Thy Word is meaningful to me. Now Thy Word is hidden in my heart. Now Thy Word is clear to me. Now I can be still long enough to meditate on Thy Word. Now I am hearing Thy Word. Now that I'm afflicted, my steps are ordered in Thy Word. Now I rejoice in Thy Word. Now I can speak boldly in Thy Word." It wasn't until I was afflicted. Now I can speak to Jesus.

I'm afflicted, now I can pray. I have been afflicted to pray. Pastor's wives, maybe you are suffering because you went astray. Maybe you are praying because you have been afflicted. Are you afflicted physically? If so, does your affliction cause inabilities, disabilities or incapabilities? Are you mentally afflicted; suffering with depression, bi-polar and the like? Is your soul afflicted; suffering with safe adultery, dainty disobedience, light stealing, small white lying, a little lust, every now and then envy, juvenile jealousy, secret pride, minute rebellion, just a hint of hatred, an ounce of anger or a spoonful of porn? Maybe you are not praying because you haven't been afflicted. Maybe you have gone astray and don't realize it. If this is so, just hold on, the day shall arise when you will be afflicted to pray.

Whatever your affliction is or whenever your affliction arises, the Bible tells us to pray. Prayer will bring you out. Cry unto the Lord; don't complain about your affliction, just pray.

To the afflicted, what is your affliction called? Can you give your affliction a name?

The David Affliction (personal sin) - David committed adultery, had the woman's husband murdered, had a baby by her, the baby was ill; David was afflicted; he fasted and prayed, the baby died, II Samuel 12.

The Jehoshaphat Affliction (holy living) - Armies came against King Jehoshaphat; he feared, fasted and prayed; God fought his battle; he became rich, II Chronicles 20.

The Satan Affliction (directly from Satan) - Job was perfect and upright; Satan stole, killed his children and burned his possessions; he worshipped the Lord; he was stricken with boils over his entire body; he never cursed God; everything Job lost was restored, Job, Chapters 1-2 and Job, Chapter 42.

The Jonah Affliction (disobedience) - detailed below.

Sometimes we don't always know how to pray about a matter, but that's okay. The Lord regards our affliction when He hears our cry, Psalm 106:44.

I struggle with teachers telling me what I need to do, but won't show me how to do it. I am a "how" person. I have to have a "how" pastor. Let me give you an example: The teacher may say study to shew thyself approved unto God, II Timothy 2:15. Okay, I can do that; that's simple. Show me how, give me some ways to do it, give me some pointers on things I may be doing that could be deterring me from studying, give me some studying tips. Some teachers say we need to do more for the Lord. I need the teacher to show me how.

I, Lady Bea, want to show you how to pray.

Jonah was directed by God to go to Nineveh to preach a word to the people. Instead, he decided to take a boat trip. He bought a ticket and went on board. The weather became inclement and because there were meteorologists on board, they knew the storm was spiritual. Jonah admitted his disobedience and was tossed overboard. Our wrongdoing affects everybody around us. We have to acknowledge it and not act as if it never happened. When we admit our sin to the Lord, He will help us. He is waiting to forgive us.

When Jonah was overthrown, the Lord prepared a great fish to swallow him up. The Lord prepared protection for him. This means when we do wrong and admit it, the Lord will prepare a protector for us to keep us safe while in our storm. We still have to suffer consequences for sinning, but we will be covered by the Lord. Jonah desired a boat ride and the Lord honored it, His way, not Jonah's way. Jonah had gone down into the sides of the ship and was fast asleep. Since he wanted to ride in the lower level of the ship and was down in the sides of the ship, the Lord fixed it up for him to be down in the sides of the fish's belly for three days and three nights.

I said all of that to get to this point. Let me show you what to pray and how to pray in your affliction.

a. Cry from the depths of thy soul, cry with your whole heart. Pray effectually and fervently. Speak to the Lord directly concerning what you have done; admit it.

Jonah cried unto the Lord by reason of his affliction in Jonah 2:2 and the Lord heard him.

b. Remember the Lord. Jonah remembered His greatness, His power, His patience, His compassion, His love, His provisions, His protection, His authority and His mercy.

Jonah talked to the Lord. Are you talking to the Lord about your affliction? He remembered the Lord. He was so weak, but had enough strength to remember to call on the Lord. He couldn't text anyone for help and neither could he Facebook anyone. He knew what to do; he was a preacher. Isn't it something how we remember the Lord in our affliction, but when we are good-timing it, the Lord is forgotten?

Jonah said the Lord cast him into the deep. Then he said he was cast out of the Lord's sight. Jonah went astray first and then he was afflicted; kind of like the psalmist; kind of like us.

c. Pray until your prayers come in unto Thee. Pray until the Lord feels your prayer, pray with faith, with boldness, with sincerity, with pure motives, with power and in Jesus' name.

Jonah said his prayer came in unto Thee. When his prayer came in unto the Lord, he knew he had reached Heaven. He knew his prayer was not only heard as in Jonah 2:2, it was felt in verse 7.

    d. Make promises unto the Lord. Promise to praise and worship, promise to serve the Lord, promise to put Jesus first before all men, all works, all possessions and keep the promises.

Jonah promised the Lord that he would sacrifice unto Him with the voice of thanksgiving and promised to keep the promise.

Pastor's wives, whatever you're faced with, know that the Lord is on your side just as He was on Jonah's side. In Jonah 2:2, the Lord heard Jonah's prayer. In verse 7, He felt Jonah's prayer and in verse 10, He answered his prayer. The Lord prepared the fish to swallow Jonah. Therefore, the fish knew the voice of the Lord's. The fish was in the water and the Bible says in Psalm 29 that the voice of the Lord is upon the waters, upon many waters and that the voice of the Lord is powerful. The Lord moved with compassion when Jonah's prayer came in unto Him. This is when the Lord spoke to the fish and then, not until then, the fish vomited out Jonah onto dry land. If the fish hears the Lord and obeys Him, why can't we? If the fish can hear the voice of the Lord upon the waters, why won't we surround ourselves with water from a fountain, swimming pool, kitchen and bathroom sink, shower or tub just to hear what thus saith the Lord? If the Lord speaks to the fish, then surely will He speak to you. Let's take advantage of the power of listening to the voice of the Lord upon the waters.

When we do anything contrary to the ways of the Lord, we forsake our own mercies. Meaning, when we do the opposite of what the Lord has directed, He will not bestow upon us His mercy. But when we repent, when we acknowledge our sin, when we are sorrowfully sorry, the Lord disperses His mercy. Mercy is our cry that the Lord hears and feels. He then moves with compassion to bless us, a little different from grace. With grace, the Lord blesses us when we're wrong, when we're unforgiving, when we're mean or selfish, when we don't even admit our error. He knows we don't deserve it, but gives us favor in spite of.

Again, is anyone afflicted? Let him pray!

Jonah was in a dark situation. He was in the belly of a fish. He was riding at the bottom of the mountains with weeds wrapped around his head; isn't that bondage. What are you trapped in? What's useless, like a weed, that's wrapped around your head? Jonah was in trouble and none of his family members and friends knew it. The last they heard was that he was taking a trip. Like you, the last your family and friends heard was that you were a pastor's wife, a pastor, a church member, a leader, an entrepreneur, an employee, or a parent. Here's my advice:

In your affliction, remember that darkness is God's secret place. If darkness is God's secret place, go into your secret closet in your dark hour and meet the Lord there. It's prayer time!

Chapter 18

"Loose My Mind, Satan!"

Strongholds:

Strongholds are yokes that bind our minds. They are thoughts that block the truth from entering in our mind, but at the same time, strongholds keep the untruth locked in our minds. Satan has a hold; we have to pull them down. Strongholds will make you think your wrong doing is right. When truth is before you, strongholds will block you from receiving it. Claxton said I didn't help him in the ministry; that was not true. There was documentation, assistance, and positive reports from the members. He still believed otherwise. Strongholds will make you believe a lie though you know the truth. Woe until him that calleth evil good and good evil, that putteth darkness for light and light for darkness and putteth bitter for sweet and sweet for bitter; these are strongholds.

Any word that is contrary to the Word of God and it is believed, is a stronghold. Strongholds are heavy; they control the mind. Many times as children, we are taught untruths by adults which become strongholds. Example: My mother always said I was pretty ugly. I thought that meant I was borderline, half pretty, half ugly. When I grew up, the term pretty ugly had stuck with me. I thought I looked okay or average because of what Mama said. Then I got revelation of what "pretty ugly" meant and thought to myself, "Mama was saying I was pretty ugly as in severely ugly." Then that stuck with me. When people began to compliment me as an adult, I would say to myself, "People need to quit lying because I know the truth." In my case, my looks were not important to me and my self-esteem was not lowered because of it. I had other low self-esteem issues. The truth of the matter could have been proven by others, but I still would have believed what Mama said.

Think about the things you think about. Are they holy or are they wicked thoughts? With strongholds, our wrong thinking is righteous thoughts to us. One may say, "My thoughts may not be holy all of the time, but they are never wicked. Another may say, "My thoughts are neither holy nor wicked, they are regular thoughts." Let's go a little deeper:

The thoughts you have, are they contrary or against the knowledge of God, the Word? Can you find your thoughts in the Bible?

Can your thoughts be written down and read by your pastor?

Can your thoughts bless someone, encourage them or lift up their bowed down head?

Can your thoughts draw someone to Jesus Christ?

The things you imagine, are they pleasing unto God?

Do you imagine yourself rich in money, prestige, and possessions or do you imagine yourself rich in wisdom, knowledge, faith, favor and understanding?

Are your thoughts of evil and not good?

If your spouse or a loved one consistently tells you what you're thinking is erroneous and they provide proof, and you're looking at the proof, but refuse to accept the truth, that's a stronghold.

Strongholds are similar to selfishness. You know the scenario of giver's hands being open to receive and to give, but the stingy person's hand stays closed, nothing entering or exiting? That's how it is with strongholds. Our minds are shut tightly by Satan, nothing comes in and nothing is going out. But with the power of Jesus, these strongholds can be pulled down by fasting and praying.

If you think alcohol gives you power, it's a stronghold. If you think fornication or adultery does the body good, it's a stronghold. The Bible calls it a dual sin; sin against our body and against the Lord. If you think over the counter or prescription drugs soothe your soul, it's a stronghold. If lying a little bit is not that bad, that's a stronghold. Cigarette smoking is a stronghold. I was a smoker of two packs per day. The devil made me think I needed a smoke in the morning, after eating, on breaks, with coffee and during many other times. I have my prayer technique the Lord gave me in detail just for you in TPWDC book. The prayer can also be used to eradicate any stronghold or habit.

Pastor's wives, sometimes we are loaded with strongholds and the pastors, too. This is what's slowing down the process of ministering to the lost. We're heavy and causing others to be weighed down and we wonder why we're not advancing the Kingdom. If your husband's characteristics were outlined in this book, consider help for him. Too many souls are leaving earth unsaved. Too many souls are lost and they are sitting in the church thinking they're safe. Too many pastors are quitting ministry or they are replaced. When you see or hear of a falling ministry, don't watch it tumble, don't watch the pastor slip, don't watch sheep scatter, don't keep quiet. Do something. Seek counsel. If the ministry's leader has been warned and he continues to stray, the blood is off of your hands.

Pastor's wives, let's keep our minds on the Word, not on the things of the world. While you're looking good, cast out a demon. Slip those gorgeous hands with the diamonds on the nails, up in the air and worship the Lord. Walk your beautiful feet, with your ever so unique shoes, over to a needy person and offer something. Sling your hair in somebody's face as you pray for them. Take your one-of-a-kind car and drive someone to the store. Take some money out of your name-brand purse and bless somebody real good. If you get your eyelashes a little longer then maybe you can carry a few lost souls to the altar during altar call.

Time is running out for us all. Pastor's wives, we are the leaders of the women. Instead of turning our plates over, we are piling them up or instead of pushing our plates back, we are pulling them toward us; we simply need to throw the plates away. Yet we wonder why we have no breakthroughs. We wonder why there are no changes in us, our homes, our marriages or our churches. We must come together. I pray that I'm helping you.

Chapter 19

Pastor and Mrs. Claxton William Morgan

I drew up the paperwork for a legal separation at Claxton's request. We met at the bank to have the papers notarized and proceeded on to the county court to file the papers. You know how you feel when a task has been completed? I was pretty excited about my "for real" freedom. I'm thinking that after it was finalized, I would be free to go meet a male in public places without feeling as if I was sinning. As ministers, we have to be careful when we're out and not with our spouses even though the meeting may be innocent. The Bible tells us not to let our good be evil spoken of. If our behavior to others or what is seen by others deters them from Christ, wisdom was not utilized. After a couple of months went by, Claxton called and said he rescinded the legal separation documents. I choked. I got sanctified and went Old Testament on him and said, "What hast thou saith?" I thought maybe I heard him wrong, so I said, "You re-sent the documents as in re-faxed?" He said, "No, I stopped the process." What could I say? What could I do? I know you're saying, "What did you say, what did you do? Well, I did nothing, I did absolutely nothing. After all of that turmoil, suffering, praying and fasting, we reunited briefly! Claxton thought I was the same young woman he married over a decade prior. I gave up my peaceful townhome the Lord blessed me with. I, as in flesh, did not want to live with him and I kept talking to the Lord about it and kept waiting for answers from the Lord. I did more meditation than ever. Claxton was so nice and he couldn't understand why I wasn't excited about getting back together. I couldn't believe that he couldn't understand why. The Lord told me to go back. I said to the Lord over and over that I didn't want to go. The Lord told me to go a final time. I said, "Lord, if this is what You want me to do, You know I am in a lease, get me out of it." I wrote a 30-day notice to the leasing office to break my lease and had planned to drop it off on the way home from church. In route to church my friend called me and asked me if she could move into my apartment because she had 30 days to move out of her home she had just lost. I added her to my lease, she moved in and I moved back with Claxton. It was just that smooth. As the movers were dropping off my furniture at the new home, Claxton was unpacking it and setting it up. He grocery shopped and was so helpful. We really didn't know each other anymore. I didn't fully trust him. I was not afraid of him. I wasn't holding any grudges. I wasn't hurt by previous matters and he was forgiven. I slept with my third eye open. I was expecting something supernatural to happen, so while I was waiting, I was just there trying to get the marriage back to the way it was when we first married. That was a struggle. I felt the spirit of being locked up or locked down in the atmosphere. I never stopped consecrating, meditating or praying at 5:00 a.m.

Guess what? He was still controlling. He had not been delivered. He controlled the thermostat and threatened to put a lock on it; that threat wasn't new. He controlled the lights. He didn't want the porch light on while I was gone at night and it was pitch black outside. He literally unscrewed the bulb and threatened to remove the bulb the next time it was left on. He parked his car either in the garage or at the very tip of the driveway so I couldn't put my car in the garage or the driveway. I parked on the street. He stopped talking to me; I mean, he just shut down completely. He'd come home from work, go into the bedroom, talk on his cell phone for hours and laugh out loud. I didn't know who he was talking to. On Sundays, I'd hear him talking about how service went and how the Lord moved that day. Please don't ask me what church he attended. I was not hurt by what was going on. I knew there was a reason for our reunion other than the restoration of our marriage. At the same time, it was as if he was a total stranger to me. I knew that a lot of work was going to have to be done, but it had to be two doing the work. I am not a fusser or a complainer and neither am I argumentative, so the things he was doing weren't phasing me. Not that I didn't care; I needed to know why I was here; not from him, but from the Lord. One day Claxton came home from work heavy laden. I saw in the spirit the weight that rested upon him as he was walking down the hallway. I had my Glory music on; a compact disc by Faith Miracle Temple Church called Soaking in the Glory, you have to get it; the website is faithmiracletemple.org. The volume was extremely low as always. The demons can't stand that music. One day I had it on low in the living room, Claxton clowned about it, saying that I was being disrespectful by blasting it and disturbing the entire household; it was all a lie. It was blasting to the demons; they couldn't take it. We had been separated so long that he had forgotten that I always kept worship music playing in my prayer room all day and all night. He went on into our bedroom and shut the door. I went into my daughter's bedroom to hide from her and I was on the phone. The kids were in the kitchen. A few minutes later I heard a loud crash. I didn't check it out to see what it was. About 15 minutes later I went into the living room and saw my oldest son cleaning up glass. I asked him what happened and he didn't know; glass was everywhere. A corner piece of glass from the top shelf of the china cabinet fell and all of my dishes and glass vases broke into tiny pieces that were sitting on the second shelf. As soon as I saw it, I knew the unclean spirits that rested on Claxton were stirred up by the music and they needed an escape. The escape was the china cabinet. I had never seen so many tiny pieces of glass. I couldn't remember what the dishes once looked like. I didn't think to open a window or a door at that time. It is imperative to play worship music in your home on low around the clock. Anyway, Claxton William Morgan stopped paying the bills. He said that he was saving his money and he was not paying anything. He said I was doing him a favor by staying with him because the longer I stayed, the more he'd save. Isn't that beautiful? I was lying in the bed one day, praying in tongues and Claxton stuck a pen in my mouth and told me to shut that noise up. I knew then I was dealing head on, with the devil. He was laughing just like a witch saying, "Listen to yourself; sounding crazy." He was just laughing. As he laughed, I was walking up and down the hallway, walking through the living room, dining room and kitchen, in a circle, praying. On my way back down the hallway this last time, Claxton stuck his head out of the kitchen doorway and I snatched his head with both of my hands and commanded demons to come off of him in the name of Jesus. I don't believe he was possessed, but oppressed. My hands were stuck to his head by the power of Jesus. Claxton wiggled like a snake, going backward all the way to the other side of the kitchen. When the Lord was ready, He detached me. When that happened, His power thrashed me into the wall; it was like lightning. I was waiting on something supernatural and I got it! Claxton got up off of the floor and went into the basement for a long time. When he finally came back upstairs, he moved out of our bedroom into our daughter's bedroom and moved her in with me. I have never shared a room with my kids. He moved all of her clothes into my closet. When I'd go into my bedroom and shut my door, who did I see? My daughter lying in my bed, watching my television with my remote control with her legs crossed, grinning, saying, "This is our room." You know how we say the devil is a liar? I don't say that anymore. I just say, "The devil is." When my daughter kept saying, "Our room, our closet and our bathroom," all I could say was, "The devil is." Remember back in Chapter 1 when Claxton said I needed a plan? I took his advice again. I moved out and did not feel bad about it. I believe the reunion was specifically for closure. I left with the joy of the Lord. Though we are in the process of a divorce, we are friends. Please note that I have learned so much from Pastor Claxton William Morgan. His teaching was with clarity and his preaching was powerful. His prayers were untouchable and Satan knew this. Prayerfully, this book encourages him to get back on his feet and continue to do the work of the Lord, but in a greater fashion, using this book as a guideline to operate his new ministry with his new family, differently.

As with all marriages, there are tests and trials to endure. To date, there has not been a perfect marriage. Therefore, when Jesus is the head of your marriage and His guidelines are followed, there is victory at the end of the road. During our trials, we must stand upon the promises of God, constantly seeking His face while awaiting direction from Jesus alone. We must remember that our trials are not to wipe us out or to knock us down, but to lift us up spiritually, humble us, give us patience and experiences. Without experiences, we are not able to testify, encourage or counsel effectively.

In essence, no matter the couple, there will be friction because Satan hates unity. Once a couple marries, Satan begins his mission which is "division." This is when couples must increase their prayer lives; learn to handle matters rationally, immediately, and spiritually; fast together; respect each other's opinions and views; learn to listen with an open mind; get an understanding; make time to spend together alone; continue to date after marriage; please each other after first pleasing the Lord; stay on one accord; allow no one to intercept the relationship, including children; develop a system to keep communication lines open; be open and honest about all matters; never give the silent treatment; deposit 100 percent of self into the relationship, not 50 percent and serve the Lord together!

Wives, do your all, even if it seems as though you're getting shortchanged. God sees it all!

Reverence your husband in spite of your dilemma. Everything we do must be done as unto the Lord. We cannot be mean or unkind to our spouse. Never let it be said that you retaliated. In my quiet time one day I was thinking about how I assist so many people, including strangers, with comfort, encouragement, giving, listening, prayer and much more. I said to the Lord, "I am tired of being nice to everybody." Have you ever felt like that? He replied, "Never get tired of being like Me." That touched me and encouraged me to do more; I desire to see His face!

If you are not rewarded on this side of the vineyard, know that your reward is coming on the other side.

Always remember that The "Pastor's Wife Does Cry!" Pray for all Pastor's wives, hurting wives, pastors, each other and please pray for me and Claxton!

I pray that something in this book was learned or grasped to enhance your life in some way!

Be blessed and know that God is on your side!

Lady Bea Morgan

Scriptures and References

The Pastor's Wife Does Cry, *Lady Bea Morgan*

Walking in Righteousness, *Brenda B. Matthews*

Humbling Thyself, *Brenda B. Matthews*

If I Were A Man And Had A Wife, *Brenda B. Matthews*

King James Version of the Holy Bible

****

Scriptures of Comfort!

This is my **comfort in my affliction**; for Your Word has **given me life**, Psalm 119:50

Many of the afflictions of the righteous; **the Lord will deliver** them out of them all, Psalm 34:19

It is good for me that I have been afflicted that I may **learn thy statutes**, Psalm 119:71

Nevertheless, he regarded their affliction when he heard their cry, Psalm 106:44

He delivereth the poor in his affliction, *and openeth their ears in oppression, Job 36:15*

*For thou wilt **save the** afflicted *people; but wilt bring down high looks, Psalm 18:27*

CPSIA information can be obtained at www.ICGtesting.com
Printed in the USA
LVOW131611120412

277373LV00006B/32/P